D1599434

Lone Star Confederate

TEXAS A&M UNIVERSITY
MILITARY HISTORY SERIES
84

Lone Star Confederate

A Gallant and Good Soldier
of the 5th Texas Infantry

EDITED BY GEORGE SKOCH
& MARK W. PERKINS

FOREWORD BY ROBERT K. KRICK

Texas A&M University Press *College Station*

WITHDRAWN

Property of
FAUQUIER COUNTY PUBLIC LIBRARY
11 Winchester Street
Warrenton, VA 20186

Copyright © 2003 by Mark William Perkins,
George Franklin Skoch, and Sharlene Warner
Manufactured in the United States of America
All rights reserved
First edition

The paper used in this book
meets the minimum requirements
of the American National Standard for Permanence
of Paper for Printed Library Materials, z39.48-1984.
Binding materials have been chosen for durability.

Library of Congress Cataloging-in-Publication Data

Campbell, Robert, b. 1844.
    Lone Star Confederate : a gallant and good soldier of the 5th Texas
Infantry / edited by George Skoch and Mark W. Perkins ; foreword by
Robert K. Krick.—1st ed.
        p. cm.— (Texas A & M University military history series ; no. 84)
Includes bibliographical references (p.) and index.
    ISBN 1-58544-238-0 (cloth : alk. paper)
    1. Campbell, Robert, b. 1844.   2. Confederate States of America.
Army. Texas Infantry Regiment, 5th.   3. United States—History— Civil
War, 1861–1865—Personal narratives, Confederate.   4. Virginia—
History—Civil War, 1861–1865—Personal narratives.   5. Texas—History—
Civil War, 1861–1865—Personal narratives.   6. United States—History—
Civil War, 1861–1865—Regimental histories.   7. Texas—History—Civil
War, 1861–1865—Regimental histories.   8. Soldiers—Texas—Biography.
I. Skoch, George F.   II. Perkins, Mark W., 1955–   III. Title.   IV. Series.
E580.55th .C36   2003
973.7'64'092—dc21   2002014491

CONTENTS

MAPS

FOREWORD

⁓

The battlefield behavior of legendary leaders and units from all across the South through four years of war wove a fabric that became the story of Robert E. Lee's redoubtable Army of Northern Virginia. No organization in that army ever won more widespread renown than Hood's Texas Brigade; none deserved more.

Texans almost universally labor under the immodest notion that nothing is quite so grand as their state, its people, and its history. Such regional jingoism, of course, is not confined to Lone Star latitudes. Texans have, however, the justly earned reputation of working harder and longer at it than most. That they should be immensely proud of the famous brigade is therefore not surprising. That so many non-Texans agree on its prowess is worthy of note.

In January, 1862, commenting on a now-long-forgotten skirmish along the Potomac River, a South Carolinian colonel wrote home to his wife: "Those Texians are number one men . . . gallant and brave." Five months later, after the Texas Brigade demolished an enemy line near Richmond to win Robert E. Lee's first great offensive battle, no less an observer than the exacting Maj. Gen. Thomas J. "Stonewall" Jackson commented: "The men who carried this position were soldiers indeed." In mid-1863 Lee himself observed that "the enemy never sees the backs of my Texans."

Perhaps the most telling compliment to the brigade came from Lee in a letter to a member of the Confederate Congress. Hood's men had proved their mettle again in a crisis at the Battle of Sharpsburg on September 17, 1862. Four days later the army commander implored a Texas senator to raise more regiments in his home state and lead them to Virginia. "I need them much," Lee wrote. "I rely upon those we have in all tight places. . . . We must have more of them."

The fame of Hood's Texas Brigade reverberates still today, but there is irony in the name. The brigade's units always included some non-Texan organizations, including troops from South Carolina, Georgia, and Arkansas at various times. The brigade's 3d Arkansas fought alongside the Texans long and well. Amazingly, postwar accounts by the Arkansans boasted of a role in what they complacently identified as the Texas Brigade—not the "Texas/Arkansas Brigade." Furthermore, Hood served as the brigade's commander for only a small fraction of its history—about five months, or a bit more than 10 percent of its career. Hood had advanced to temporary division command (with his old brigade among the division's components) by August, 1862. Soon thereafter he acceded to permanent division command, and by late 1863 he was permanently separated from the old brigade by both rank and geography. Nonetheless, it is as Hood's Texas Brigade that the 1st, 4th, and 5th Texas Infantry marched into history, accompanied by other attached units at various times.

Establishing with precision the identity of the best brigade in the Army of Northern Virginia probably is too subjective an undertaking to be meaningful. Students of the war regularly tilt at such windmills, knowing full well the impossibility of finding a solid answer. Were I pressed to make such a designation, the Texas Brigade would be my choice. All of my historical endeavors, stretching back now for a third of a century, have been spent on Virginia troops. Stonewall Jackson seems to me to be surpassingly interesting, and his old brigade particularly fascinating. The prowess of the Stonewall Brigade came early, however, and faded early under the inexorable effect of bloody battlefield attrition. From June, 1862, to the fall of 1864, the Texas Brigade represented Lee's most reliable unit of that size.

The record of the Texas Brigade has spawned a tremendous body of published literature over the years, among it a flurry of recollections, letters, and narrative histories. What seems to me to be the best Confederate novel of the war, matchlessly better than the feeble modern efforts launched in that vein, is about the brigade—John W. Thomason's *Lone Star Preacher* (New York, 1941; still in print from Texas A&M).

The most valuable items in the gratifying flood of Texas Brigade material are those from the pens of participants, eyewitness accounts of the events that made the brigade famous. This book is another such source, and a very strong contribution to the literature on the Texans. Robert Campbell fought with the 5th Texas in the early baptism by fire at Eltham's Landing; during the Seven Days Campaign, including the impossible but successful charge at Gaines's Mill; and in the overwhelming attack at Second Manassas that slaughtered a detachment of New York Zouaves.

Campbell's vivid narrative benefits tremendously from its timing: he wrote his account less than four years after the events he described. Late-life memoirs suffer so often from the frailties of human memory that historians rely more on contemporary diaries and letters. Those formats, however, almost invariably are slender in length, terse in language, and devoted largely to subjects other than what interests us most. A thoughtfully composed reminiscence, directed consciously at the most important and dramatic events by a nimble-minded veteran, provides the best content. Such a focused memoir, written early rather than late, provides a riveting look at the fascinating experiences not long past. Messrs. Skoch (an accomplished Civil War cartographer) and Perkins have prepared a fine slice of Texan Confederate history.

—Robert K. Krick
Fredericksburg, Virginia

PREFACE

If Robert Campbell had gotten his way, this book would not have been published. When he sat down in 1866 to tell his story of the "Southern Revolution," this much-wounded veteran of Hood's Texas Brigade intended it for the eyes of his family and close friends, "not for the perusal of a stranger eye."

For more than a century Campbell's journal remained just as he had wished. It became a family legacy and eventually was tucked away in a box and forgotten by succeeding generations. Finally, in summer, 1970, Sharlene Davis, then a high-school-aged history buff, pulled a thick, leather-bound ledger from among a musty residue of old books stored in a relative's home in Hattiesburg, Mississippi. Sharlene was thrilled. "I just thought it was wonderful to have a real antique and something from my family's past," she recalled. Both of her parents had been orphans, and she relished this connection to an earlier generation.

This link to another era can be traced to San Angelo, Texas, and the wedding of Robert Campbell's daughter, Pauline, to Dr. L. W. Bayne, a young physician originally from Hattiesburg, about the summer of 1904. Sharlene's orphaned mother was adopted into the Bayne family. Over time the journal and other keepsakes, including a thick scrapbook that Robert Campbell and other family members had filled with memorabilia, found their way back to Hattiesburg, Mississippi, where Sharlene rediscovered them and maintained possession.

Fast forward about fifteen years. Sharlene, now a resident of Cleveland Heights, Ohio, learned of the interest one of the editors had in the Civil War at a neighborhood gathering and asked him if he would like to see an "old Civil War book" she had. But instead of the expected centennial edition of a Bruce Catton book or some coffee-table history of the war packed with Matthew Brady photographs, Sharlene appeared with a brown-paper bundle from which she removed Robert Campbell's original ledger book.

A glance at the handwriting on the title page introduced "Robert Campbell, Co A, 5th Texas Vols, Hood's Texas Brigade, Fields Division, Longstreet's Corps, Army Northern Virginia." A look between the covers quickly revealed page after page of neatly scripted lettering, clearly the work of a very literate, very capable writer. Campbell's narrative marked him as a keen observer. With the ground-level perspective of the combat infantryman, Campbell's pen captured the details of camp life, the toilsome hours on the line of march, and the chaotic ebb and flow of the battlefield. What a treasure the journal was. But there was more.

Sharlene also possessed a thick scrapbook that Robert Campbell and other members of his family had filled with memorabilia. Together, the contents of the journal and the scrapbook deftly form as complete a picture of Robert Campbell's role during the "Southern Revolution" as one might wish for.

Campbell titled his writing "A brief retrospect of my soldier days in the 'Southern Revolution' 1862–1863–1864–1865." Clearly he intended to write about the entire period of the war, but the handwritten journal traces only his first eight months as a soldier. After the last words of the journal that are published here, there is a notation, written in a different ink, "(NOTE) Left off writing the latter part of March 1866, and resumed the." And with that half-finished notation, it ends. Campbell lived twenty-six years after he started to write his story, so it seems he had time enough to continue it. We can only speculate on why the reminiscence was never finished. Campbell did relocate at about the time he began it. Perhaps he was busy with life and never took the time to continue his writing.

Campbell had supplemented the handwritten journal with a variety of documents and newspaper clippings, which he pasted in the first several pages of the ledger book. He wrote a note for each piece to explain its significance. Several letters from this source are included in this volume to fill in a bit more of his story, as are other documents by Campbell.

The editors have left Robert Campbell's writing pretty much as he wrote it. His grammar and spelling, though not perfect, need no apology. These have been left per the original. For the infrequent occurrences where Campbell's handwriting could not be deciphered, the phrase in question has been replaced by ellipsis points. On those occasions where Campbell inadvertently left out a word, the editors have added it to the text in brackets. Though the original manuscript was written in solid blocks of text with no breaks for paragraphs, the editors have broken the text into paragraphs to enhance readability. Campbell's simple chapter headings (for example, "Chapter 1") have been supplemented with a subheading that gives the principal event covered in the chapter; this was done solely to aid the reader in placing Campbell's story in the overall context of the war. Endnotes have been used for three purposes—to support, correct, or elaborate on statements of fact; to provide a little more substance to the characters named by Campbell; or to explain ideas and terms, the understanding of which Campbell might have taken for granted. In all cases, the editorial contributions are made with the sole intent of supporting Robert Campbell's telling of his story.

The editors acknowledge that a work of this nature does not happen without a great deal of assistance. Here, it is impossible to show enough gratitude to Sharlene Warner (formerly Sharlene Davis), who brought Robert Campbell's writing to light. Not only did she provide a treasure to work with, she allowed us to borrow a family heirloom for an embarrassingly long time. We also thank our families for their support and for indulging us in spending so much time in the past. The community of Civil War historians has been remarkably helpful with their encouragement and advice. Our special thanks go out to Robert K. Krick and Martin F. Graham for their material contributions to this work and to Gordon Rhea and John C. "Jack" Waugh for their suggestions and thoughtful consideration of what we were intending to do. To Robert E. L. Krick and Martin L. Callahan, we are grateful for the material they sent us. A number of institutions responded to queries and provided assistance. Chief among them we would like to thank the Cleveland Public Library, the University of Akron's Bierce Library, the Kent State University Library, the Cuyahoga County Public Library system, and the Akron-Summit County Public Library system for the use of their facilities and assistance in obtaining material through interlibrary loan. Thanks also go out to Stephen C. Stappenbeck and the Center for American History at the University of Texas at Austin, to the anonymous online librarians at the Texas State Library for their assistance in obtaining microfilms of the wartime Houston newspapers, and to the University of Virginia Library Reference and Information Services Department for their assistance in obtaining reference material. To the people at Texas A&M University Press, we offer the utmost thanks for their work in bringing this volume to its final form. Lastly, and perhaps most importantly, we thank Robert Campbell for giving us this retrospect of his soldier days.

INTRODUCTION

⌒

Robert Campbell penned an introduction to his handwritten reminiscence. It does the job well. Campbell, however, was writing for an audience who knew him. For those of us whom he foresaw picking up his story, the "others than those whom I love," an introduction to the man and the setting may be appropriate.

We do not know very much about Robert Campbell. Even the ancestor who owns the manuscript cannot tell us about him. We do know his father was also named Robert—Robert C. Campbell. The elder Campbell was born in Maryland, had lived in Mississippi and Kentucky, and then moved to Texas during the early days of its statehood.[1] He was one of many immigrants, both foreign born and U.S. citizens, who began a new life in the wide-open state. Robert C. Campbell settled in Houston, where he raised a family and practiced law. He went on to own a plantation along the Brazos River and to become a judge in Huntsville, Texas, before the Civil War. His family had at least four sons, his namesake being the eldest. There were also at least two daughters. Another child is identified by Campbell simply as "the baby."

The younger Robert Campbell was born during the time his family was in Houston, about 1844. At the start of the war, he was a student in Louisiana. He describes himself as "unaccustomed to any kind of work—raised in all the comforts and luxuries of a happy and comfortable home." Campbell seems to have been a well-respected young man, for his peers selected him to be captain of the volunteer company they raised to go to war. The school faculty aborted that mission before it started. Campbell then tried to enlist on his own, and his father denied that effort.

By early 1862, though, the South had come to realize that it was not in a ninety-day war. The younger Campbell, now eighteen, again sought to enlist, and the elder Campbell let him go. Military documents describe the new recruit as five foot, eight inches tall, with dark eyes and hair and a dark complexion.[2]

The unit Campbell enlisted with was Company A, 5th Texas Infantry Regiment. The company had its origins in a prewar militia unit known as the Bayou City Guards. It was made up of young men from the Houston area and was one of ten companies in a regiment of men from eastern Texas. The regiment was one of three from Texas that formed the core of the Texas Brigade in the Army of Northern Virginia.[3] Except for the recent recruits, the Texans had been in Virginia since the fall of the previous year. Campbell joined them just in time for their first major combat action at Eltham's Landing, Virginia.

There is information indicating Campbell carried the newly sewn 5th Texas battle flag from Texas to the regiment in Virginia when he joined the unit.[4] The details of the flag's story from a variety of sources are sketchy and confusing. Most accounts of the banner's manufacture and delivery indicate it was sent to the unit in May, 1862, and presented to the regiment in June.[5] Those dates, if correct, are too late for Robert Campbell to have taken the flag with him, for he arrived in Virginia in April of that year. But a letter to the editor of a Houston newspaper from "One of the Fifth," written in Houston on March 5, 1865 (presumably by a member of the command home on furlough, tempting one at least to wonder if Campbell, who was home on furlough at the time, had taken up the pen), solicits the manufacture of a battle flag to replace the battle-scarred banner recently returned to its maker in Houston.[6] The author of this letter describes the original flag as having been sent to the unit "over three years ago," which would place it en route at least a week before Campbell enlisted.

Aside from the reunion articles, the accounts of the 5th Texas battle flag offer no details on how it made the trip from Texas to Virginia. That Campbell did not write anything of carrying the flag to the unit seems strange if he did indeed do it. But he makes no mention of a flag-presentation ceremony known to have occurred in June, 1862, an event important enough that Campbell might have been expected to describe it. He clearly did not attempt to chronicle everything that happened, so his silence on the flag does not assure us that he was not involved.

It was mid-April, 1862, by the time Robert Campbell got to Virginia and early May by the time of the fight at Eltham's Landing.[7] Campbell would march with the 5th Texas back toward Richmond, fight some more, and then march to Manassas. At the Second Battle of Manassas, on August 30, 1862, he was wounded, shot twice in the same leg, and put out of action for a time.

Campbell was hospitalized in Virginia for a while and then furloughed back to Texas; it is his experiences to this point that he writes about. By the time it was done, Campbell's furlough had lasted approximately one year. He returned to his unit in time to leave Robert E. Lee's Army of Northern Virginia and go west to fight in another major battle at Chickamauga, Georgia. Campbell was again wounded, this time in the leg and arm. Hospitalized once more, Campbell was furloughed in Virginia and then Selma, Alabama.

When Campbell returned to service in December, 1863, he rejoined his company, now in Tennessee. Fairly incapacitated by his wounds but feeling duty bound to remain in the service of his country, Robert Campbell sought reassignment out of the infantry. A family friend wrote a letter to Jefferson Davis recommending that the Texan be appointed to a staff position.[8] A notation written on the outside of the letter reads: "Richmond, Jan. 23, 1864. I know him to be a gallant & good soldier. J. B. Hood, Maj. Genl."

Campbell did obtain an appointment as a courier at brigade headquarters in February, 1864. His scrapbook contains evidence that while on this assignment, he was a witness close at hand to one of the most famous moments of the Civil War—Robert E. Lee's attempt to personally lead the Texas Brigade into battle at the Wilderness. Pasted in the scrapbook are two clippings from newspapers that mention the "Lee at the Wilderness" incident. Beneath one, an undated letter written by E. C. Wharton of *The Orleanian,* Campbell penned a note that the account was "in the main correct, but there are two or three errors that for my own pleasure I shall here proceed to correct." The other clipping, by Campbell himself, is a letter to the editor of a newspaper identified as the *Times-Democrat* dated October 3, 1887. He wrote the letter to make a point about the high casualty rate of the Texas Brigade at the Wilderness. In doing so, Campbell states that the Lee incident occurred during the brigade's advance. By the time the brigade was ordered back, he was the only courier remaining at Brig. Gen. John Gregg's disposal out of ten or more who had started the battle, the others having been killed or wounded except for two who had been sent back to have ordnance brought up. There is clear, though circumstantial, evidence that Robert Campbell wrote the often quoted first-hand account of the "Lee to the Rear" incident first printed in the late-nineteenth-century veterans' publication *The Land We Love*. The account was written by an author identified only as "R.C." (It is included in the letters section of this work with an explanation of the case for Robert Campbell being "R.C.")

Campbell supplied his own horse for his role as a courier, and on September 29, 1864, his mount was killed in action at the Battle of Fort Harrison. For that loss, Campbell sought and, after a letter-writing campaign, was successful in receiving $1,000 compensation.

A week after losing his mount in action, Campbell received his most serious injuries of the war at Darbytown Road, Virginia, on October 7, 1864. There he was struck in the head, knee, and body. Furloughed once again, Campbell returned to Texas, evidently with more than the war on his mind. In a letter that Campbell was going to carry back to Texas, another soldier in the regiment wrote: "I want to predict that Bob Campbell is on his knees to Miss Semmons in less than no time after his arrival home. He is ready to fall in love with her at first sight."[9]

Campbell was assigned to recruiting duty in Houston after he recovered from his wounds. In early April, 1865, as the war was ending in the East, he finally wrote a letter seeking permission to retire due to his wounds; the letter is pasted in the ledger book. Although a medical examining board in Texas agreed that Campbell should be relieved from infantry duty, at the end of the war, he was listed on the last muster roll of the 5th Texas Infantry as being on furlough. In the scrapbook is a letter to Campbell from a Confederate command in San Antonio, Texas, which authorized Campbell to raise a mounted unit, but it was too late to bring the young veteran back into service.

Campbell did not stay in Texas long following the end of the war. By 1867, he had taken up residence in Yazoo City, Mississippi, the area from which his father had emigrated. Campbell led an active and admired life in Yazoo City. On November 14, 1867, he married Pauline Wilson. The couple went on to have at least five children. Scrapbook clippings indicate that at least two died in infancy and that the old soldier was survived by five children. In a margin note in the scrapbook, Campbell writes that he was living in Owensboro, Kentucky, and owned a newspaper there in 1875. Clippings and steamer passes in the scrapbook show that in 1876 he was still with the newspaper in Owensboro. Other passes dated that same year identify him as editor of the newspaper in Yazoo City, and it is in the latter town that Campbell lived out his life.

As a member of the community in Yazoo City, Robert Campbell attained a reputation as a leader and a fighter for the rights of the local citizenry in the reconstructed South. He was a member of the Episcopal church, a fireman, a Knight of Pythias, and a county clerk. He worked as editor of the *Yazoo Valley Democrat,* and he was an officer and active member of the county camp of Confederate veterans.

A respected leader of the community, Robert Campbell was called upon occasionally to speak to the populace. On October 19, 1892, he was doing just that, at a concert honoring the first anniversary of the Yazoo City Concert Band. Finishing his remarks, which were, as always, well received, Campbell began to feel faint. Friends at the hall assisted him to his home one block away. There he told his wife he felt tired and admonished his daughter that she "must be a good girl." With that said, Robert Campbell quietly passed away.[10]

The military organization Campbell belonged to was one of the most renowned in all the world. Robert E. Lee's Army of

Northern Virginia fought for three years against a succession of Union generals leading a much larger and much better-supplied force. Elite among this elite army was the Texas Brigade, identified most often with its third and most famous commander, John Bell Hood.

Texans were marching to war in the East before there was a Texas Brigade. As hostilities began to look inevitable, citizens in Texas prepared for war. The state answered a call for troops in April, 1861. While concerned about protecting her own borders, both from the new threat of the United States and the continuing danger from hostile Indians, the proud Texans also wanted to show their fellow Confederates that Texans could fight. Several companies of troops began to make their way to Virginia. The first few to arrive were rushed to Manassas in July, 1861, for the first major battle of the war but arrived after the fighting was over. Nevertheless, these first arrivals would become the 1st Texas Infantry Regiment.

Additional volunteers enlisted in Texas following a call for troops on June 30, 1861. Approximately two thousand of these new soldiers also made their way to Virginia during the late summer and fall of that year. On September 30 they became the 4th and 5th Texas Infantry Regiments. The three regiments provided the Texas component of the Texas Brigade in the Virginia army. They were commanded by Louis T. Wigfall. He gave way to James J. Archer, who in a matter of days gave way to John Bell Hood.

In November, 1861, the 18th Georgia Infantry Regiment was assigned to Hood's brigade. It and the three Texas regiments formed the brigade when Campbell joined it. He had been recruited in March, 1862, by a detail sent back home from the brigade to gather more men. Campbell enlisted on March 14, 1862.

On June 1, 1862, the infantry portion of Hampton's South Carolina Legion was assigned to the brigade. A battery of North Carolina artillery was also attached to the brigade during the summer of 1862. Thus composed, the brigade fought in the battles around Richmond and at Manassas and then marched into Maryland, an invasion that culminated in the battle at Sharpsburg (Antietam) in September. By then Hood had been promoted to command the division that the Texas Brigade belonged to. Even so, he had been so well liked by the men that they continued to refer to themselves as "Hood's Brigade." His successor commanding the brigade was William T. Wofford of the 18th Georgia.

Lee reorganized his army in November, 1862, assigning regiments from the same state together. The Georgia and South Carolina troops were reassigned. But since there were no other Texas troops in Lee's army, the lone Arkansas regiment in the army, the 3d Arkansas, was assigned to the Texas Brigade. Command of the brigade was given to Jerome B. Robertson of the 5th Texas.

The Texans were not very heavily involved in the battle at Fredericksburg in December, 1862. In April, 1863, the brigade was sent with the rest of James Longstreet's command to the Suffolk, Virginia, area, where they were to keep Federal troops in the area checked and to forage for badly needed supplies for Lee's army. Longstreet's troops rejoined Lee just after the Battle of Chancellorsville. In June they began marching north once again. As was often the case, the Texas Brigade was assigned the vital and dangerous task of providing the rear guard for the marching column. This invasion ended with the July battle at Gettysburg, Pennsylvania, which was also the last battle in which Reilly's North Carolina Artillery fought with the brigade.[11]

Following the army's return to Virginia, the Texas Brigade once again was detailed away from the army as part of Longstreet's command. They helped defeat the Federals at Chickamauga, then unsuccessfully laid siege to Union forces at Knoxville. Following an unusually hard winter, which magnified the poor condition of their uniforms and supplies, the brigade returned to Virginia and Lee's army. Robertson was transferred out of the command in February, 1864, and replaced by another Texan, John Gregg. During the spring and summer of 1864, the Texans participated in all the battles between Lee and Grant. They fought fiercely and played particularly critical roles at both the Wilderness and Spotsylvania Court House. Later in the year the brigade took to the trenches with the rest of the army in the Richmond-Petersburg area.

On October 7, 1864, Gregg was killed at Darbytown Road—the same battle at which Campbell received his last wounds of the war. Frederick S. Bass took command of the brigade. He later relinquished command to a senior colonel, Robert M. Powell, a recently returned prisoner of war who had commanded the 5th Texas at Gettysburg, where he was captured. Powell led the brigade for the remainder of the war.[12] When Lee surrendered the Army of Northern Virginia at Appomattox Court House in April, 1865, there were only some six hundred men left out of the more than five thousand who had served in the four regiments making up the final roster of Hood's Texas Brigade.

Lone Star Confederate

Chapter 1

ENLISTMENT

*I*t is but proper that in writing this which savors so much of egotism, that I should briefly digress at the start and explain the object of my writing – in order to obviate any unjust conclusions being formed against myself. Everyone is moved by a spirit of pride and self-satisfaction, at every undertaking, which when completed, merits the commendation – *well done.* When an individual commences a task, and at its "finis," feels within himself that he has performed it *to the best of his ability,* he is surely deserving of praise – for in encouragement of that task, to the memory of which these pages are dedicated, I *feel* within myself, that I have performed to the best of my ability *all* duties that devolved upon me – cheerfully and willingly – and feeling no prickings of conscience for past neglect – I can with more self-satisfaction – write concerning myself – what I have seen – felt, and experienced in the bloody drama of war.

The War has ended, disaster and failure have crowned the *noble, gallant, self-sacrificing* efforts of the Southern people for their gov-

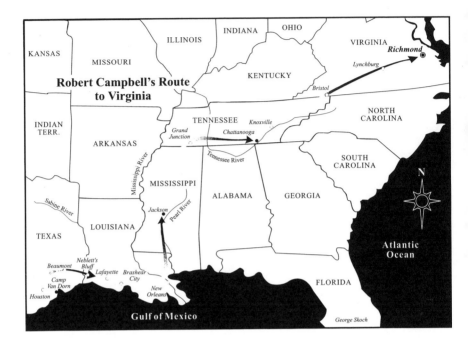

ernment and in this hour of gloom tis no pleasing task to dwell upon a picture which but reflects sad memories of the past – and gloomy anticipation for the future. Tis but a natural conclusion, that since the Yankees look upon us as a conquered and vile race that they will veto the publication of a history of this war by Southern talent and especially where that history wears the garb of truth – hence the best history of the past bloody days will be found in the memories – notebooks and letters of those who figured in the scenes – for this reason have I written upon this topic at all. Why there's so much of egotism about the composition I also will explain. In the first place, this "retrospect" is written only for the eyes of those who are most dear to me, by ties of consanguinity and friendship – and not for the perusal of a stranger eye – and in case this should be read – by others than those whom I love, take to yourselves the explanations I have proffered. My memory can *now* with more correctness than at a later period, retrace the footprints of four eventful years and while thus fresh – I desire to jot down the acts and recollections of those years. In years to come – when memory begins to fail – it will be to me a pleasure to peruse these pages. To those who love me – these homely lines will prove of interest. The egotism, which is so glaring – is easily accounted for – since what is written, is for my pleasure of those who love me. These alone – and who, when reading it will not read to learn concerning the *war*, but to go – in fancy, oer the scenes of my youthful days – and though were I to intrude these lines upon the notice of *passing* friends, I would deserve to be rated among the most accomplished charlatans. Yet, rest assured, but few will receive from *me* an invitation to read these dull – and homely revelations – rather remembrances – of the past.

In a composition like this, without a single note, without the aid of a single individual – conversant from experience with the issues here narated – with nothing but memory to narate acts *long since* past, it is but natural that mistakes as to *exact* dates – together with the topographys of places, will now and then occur – yet in the main, truth and correctness shall mark my narrative. With these few explanatory remarks and many requests for indulgence I begin a truthful tale which had its rise and fall with "bloody war."

At the breaking out of the Southern War (20) twenty companies were accepted by President Davis for the "Virginia" then known as "Army of the Potomac."[1] Nor was it without difficulty that Texas could obtain the privilege of being represented in Virginia – for victory having blessed our armies at the 1st Manassas battle. The whole country proud and defiant, but were delusively lulled into the belief that a few weeks would see us free and independent with but little actual war – fallacious reasoning. Laboring under this phantasy, the greatest eagerness prevailed among the companies . . . on Virginia soil, fearing that the War would end ere they had had a chance to see the Hessian foe, but ask them now if their fond hopes have been realized and if they have yet met in bloody encounter, their country's enemy, and they will point with emotions of sorrow to the many "green mounds" from "Elthams Landing" to "Appomattox Court House,"[2] where gallant spirits lie – "sleeping the sleep that knows no wakening." The month of October 1861 – found the 20 companies camped around Richmond. They were organized and designated as 4th and 5th Texas Vols. Capt. J. J. Archer[3] – an old U.S. officer was made Col. of the 5th. Capt. J. B. Robertson[4] commanded one of the companies from Washington County, Texas and a "revolutionary Texan" was made Lt. Col. Capt.

Brown Botts,[5] Capt. of the company from Houston, Harris County Texas was made major. Lt. Keen[6] from Washington County – adjutant.

The 4th was organized by J. B. Hood[7] – a Lt. in the U.S.A. and an adopted Texan being made Col. John Marshall[8] from Austin, Texas was Lt. Col. Warwick,[9] a Virginian, was made Major. The 20 companies – (which I will now call 4th & 5th) found on their arrival in Virginia, a Texas regiment known as 1st Texas Vols. commanded by Col. Lewis T. Wigfall,[10] U.S. senator from Texas at time of secession. The 1st Texas was comprised of companies who in their ardor and love of country had left Texas on their own had paid their way and organized on their arrival. After the 4th & 5th were organized, we were united with the first Texas and 18th Georgia – and were placed under the command of Col. Wigfall – Now – Brigadier Gen. commanding "Texas Brigade." Soon after, the Brigade was ordered to the Potomac – and stationed near Dumfries where they built Winter Quarters – lived well and had much sickness becoming aclimated. While no fighting [occurred] the muster rolls of the three Texas Regts showed at least 3000 names. During the winter (61) Genl. Wigfall having been elected Senator from Texas, took his seat in the Confederate Senate. Col. Hood – 4th Texas was made Brig. Genl. Marshall was made Col. 4th. Warwick – Lt. Col. and Capt. Keys[11] Co "A" 4th Texas became Major.

I will now turn to myself, show where I was and when connected with the Brigade. When the War broke out, I was in Louisiana at school. The students raised a company and I was honored with the office of Capt. Knowing that every young man should be found at the front, we were about to discuss the plan of offering our services to Gov. Moor[12] of La. – when the faculty learning of it – broke the company up. I then sought my fathers permission to join the army – this he refused on account of my youth (being just 17) and believing that the war would last but a few months and for that short space – not desiring my studies to be broken into. I returned home (summer 61) where I remained until the beginning of the Spring of 62 – suffering much mental agony – on account of being kept from the field – feeling, knowing that I should be in my country's service and desiring it above all things. In March 1862 Lieut. James Clute[13] of Co. "A" 5th Texas came home (Houston,

Texas) after recruits. Perceiving that Lincoln and the Yankee Govt. were determined on coercion – my father cheerfully gave his son to this country's cause, lamenting that he had but one old enough to go. I was sworn into Co. "A" 5th Texas Vol. March 12th 1862. Well, yea, very well, do I remember the day when first I clad myself in my suit of "Rebel grey" – and went around biding friends adieu. It was the proudest day of my life, and though but 17 years old, young – inexperienced – unaccustomed to *any kind* of work – raised in all the comforts and luxuries of a happy and comfortable home – I went forth – willing – ready, yea anxious to do anything that would serve the interests of my dearly loved country. Lt. Clute, myself and some 15 young men – all anxious to do and dare, who had involved their names upon Co "A"s muster roll, left Houston for Virginia about the middle of April. On our route, the whole country seemed up and ready for conflict. Our noble women vied with one another in sending their kindered to battle. On our arrival in New Orleans – we heard of the fall of Fort Donelson and Fort Henry.[14] We arrived in Richmond the latter part of April 1862.

Chapter 2

YORKTOWN

*O*n our arrival in Richmond, we were informed that Genl. Joseph E. Johnston,[1] who was comndg. "Army of Potomac"[2] had marched from the Potomac to the Virginia Peninsula and was in the neighborhood of Yorktown on the York river, confronted by Genl. George B. McLelland[3] – who was comndg. the Yankee Army – to use a Yankee phrase *"The finest under the Sun."* The truth of which assertion, I will discuss in time. In Richmond we obtained "Enfield Rifles"[4] (with which my regt. was armed) haversacks – knapsacks – blankets – and canteens – drew two days rations – and Lieut. Clute with his fifteen rebels started for Yorktown. We took the "Richmond and Yorktown RR" – as far as York river (20 miles) at which place in a heavy rain we took a schooner for Yorktown – at which place we landed about dark – wet and worn out – and having then some four miles to walk. It was now about the 15th of April 62. We found the "Texas Brigade" camped some four miles from Yorktown – on the outpost reserve line – doing picket duty –

{ 8 }

scouting and sharpshooting. My comp. numbered at least 80 men fit for duty besides some 50 more – absent sick and on detached service.[5] As soon as we arrived in camp, the rain began to pour down and our more veteran comrades shared their supplies and tents with us – rather their "brush holes" – known in military circles by the title of "Shebang" – This then was soldiering. Where were the tents – with every comfort – provisions of all kind – which I had in my ignorance imagined belonged to soldiers life? *This was war* and in it – I was to learn by experience what want and suffering meant. The boys were all in fine spirits and even for the fray – never yet having smelt powder. I found myself the youngest – by two years in the company – and the more experienced, aged – and ro-bust – prognosticated that I would soon "*cave*" either from disease or weakness of constitution. I went to work – with some ten others – and we soon had us up a capacious shebang and resolved our-selves into a "*Mess No* 10."[6] I will now turn to the affairs of general interest. We remained in our camp until the 4th of May. Nothing important transpiring on account of the bad weather – it having been raining for nearly two weeks. Our army numbered so far as I could learn some 25,000 men.[7] It became evident to Genl. Joe Johnston that the peninsula could not be held since we were con-fronted by a powerful – well disciplined – and well supplied army, which difficulty we could perhaps have overcome, had not both our flanks been uncovered by navigable streams, right and left, on each of which the enemy had powerful fleets, to which we could oppose nothing, consequently they could land forces in our rear most any time.

On the night of May 3rd orders came to be ready to march at day light – and on the morning of May 4th Johnston's army took up the line of march for Williamsburg – *retreating*. The "Texas Bri-gade" left camp by 8 A.M. – the rear guard of the "Virginia Army" – the 5th Texas bringing up the entire rear. The Yanks would have remained for many hours in ignorance of this move, had not our magazine in Yorktown been blown up – *contrary to orders*. Every sign indicated active and bloody work. McLelland was preparing to put down the rebellion. Williamsburg was 12 miles distant from our camp – we (rear guard) reached it by 5 P.M. (May 4th 62) Every 5 minutes during the day – we would be halted – deploy ourselves as skirmishers, or form squares to receive the advance of the Yanks – who were hot in pursuit, but we never engaged them.[8] On our arrival at Williamsburg – we saw some six Brigades[9] – in line of battle just this side (1/2 mile) and all the forts which had been built by Magruder[10] – strongly manned and prepared for action. "What's up?" – ran along the lines. We marched through them and entered the principle street of this old colonial town – colors flying and drums beating. Even at this late day, the sadness then felt comes vividly to mind. The tearful faces of Virginia daughters, the sorrow and gloom manifest in the countenances of old and young, made the blush of shame mount each soldier's brow, that *we* should be compelled to fall back from the Yanks – and surrender it to the vandal foe, the beautiful town of Williamsburg – with it's true and noble denizens. But "our country" demanded – and we made the sacrifice. We camped 3 miles beyond Williamsburg – and hungry – tired – and foot sore – we sank to sleep.

By 3 A.M. (May 5th) we were aroused – and in a pelting rain – and impenetrable darkness we began a hurried march. We had of late been united to Whitings Brigade – forming a "sub-division" under the command of Genl. Whiting[11] and of Genl. Gustavus W. Smith's[12] Army Division. About 7 A.M. on the march – heavy and continued firing was heard – which we were informed later in the day – came from the bloody field of "Williamsburg." We had awaited their coming and after a desperate fight of five hours "Old Joe" flogged them. That night (5th) our visionous boys gave up Williamsburg.

On the night of May 4th, Genl. Johnston received reliable information that "Little Mac" had sent 25,000 men under Major Gen. Franklin[13] up York River, in transports – to land at "Elthams Landing," alias, "West Point," (the terminus of the "Richmond and York River R.R.") by which movement, if successful, our entire army would be cut off from Richmond (our base) our artillery – ordinance and provision train captured – and Richmond be entirely unprotected. Our measures had to be executed, and *promptly* too – and to this do we owe our early rise and hurried march – in darkness – rain – mud & water. By the night of the 6th (May) we had reached the neighborhood of "West Point." Concerning this march, allow me to make a few brief remarks. During the entire two days the rain came in torrents. Mud was knee deep, wagons – canon – and mules were boging and breaking down. Soldiers – exhausted and sick were strung along the route. This was my first experience in hardships. I stood the march from Yorktown – bravely keeping up all the time, but on the evening of May 5th – nature refused to carry me further and near 5 P.M. in company with Paul McCullan[14] – one of the company – I lay by on the wood pile – sick – footsore, wet – hungry – and broke down. We repaired to a neighboring residence where we found some 15 other "Rebs" situated as we were. The residence belonged to Capt. Gaddy of the Virginia "Cavalry" and his noble and patriotic wife and daughters (God bless them), kindly took us in – placed us in the cellar by a rousing fire – dried our clothes – and gave us a delicious meal – of cornbread and bacon. I slept that night upon a bench – and sweetly did I rest. I woke by daylight – prepared to resume my march and rejoin my command. I was much refreshed. McCullan I found unable to go having a high fever I shouldered my rifle showered my gratitude on Mrs. Gaddy and her daughters – loaned "Gay Paul" $5.00 – gave him my blessing – and began again to plough the mud – in company with a thousand stragglers like myself. I continued my tramp during the entire day and having an empty haversack, I feasted on anticipations. The woods were knee-deep in mud & water and I tracked Whitings Sub Division – by many stragglers – broken down wagons – "played out" mules – and browning rails made into fires by the boys in their short halts. By 4 P.M. it cleared off beautifully and by 6 P.M. I ran upon the Brigade camped for the night. We were now in a short distance of "West Point," the point for which we had been so hurriedly marching – in order to receive in "style" Major Genl. Franklin and his 25,000 escort. During the entire night (May 6th) stragglers were pouring into camp. By daylight all were in. The day of May 7th was ushered into existence – crowned with all the beauties of nature. The sun shown clear and cheerfully. The clouds had all dispersed – birds of sweet song were everywhere heard – warbling in the sweetest tones. What a contrast to scenes about to transpire in a few hours?

We (Whitings Div) were aroused and placed under arms at 5 A.M. The 1st & 4th Txs – 18th Ga. were immediately marched off and stationed near the point of landing. Whitings own Brigade

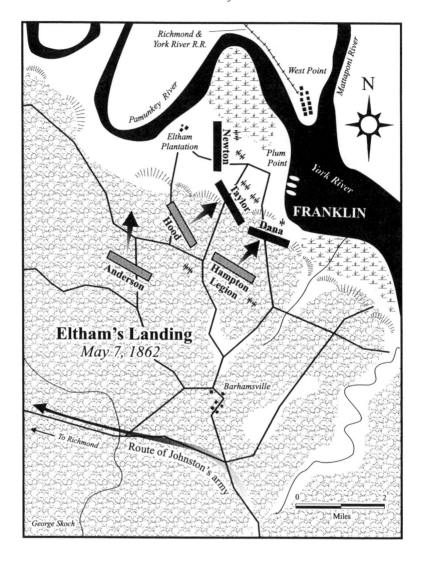

commanded by Col Law[15] of Ala. was stationed as a reserve. They had been absent an hour when we (5th Txs) were started on the march. We went 1/2 mile and were halted at a "corn crib" and two ears of hard corn issued to each man, a poor nourishment for men who had been two days fasting. We then were double-quicked by Col Archer for nearly a mile and formed a line of battle. We moved in this order into a cape of woods. Our position was about 1/2 mile above the other troops and we were stationed there to protect the

left flank. We had halted but a few moments when we were about
faced and double quicked back to "night camp." Had we remained
10 minutes longer we would have been cut off as a body of Yanks
had landed first below us and were moving on a line directly between us and the other regts. As we reached our old camp – loud
peals of musketry greeted our ears – *not* more than a mile off the
battle of "*West Point*" had begun.[16] Col. Archer ordered us towards
the firing at a double quick and after we had advanced a half mile
we were halted and the order "load at will" – was given – we were
soon loaded – capped – and ready for the fray. We now struck the
main road leading to "West Point" – and proceeding down it – to
within 1/2 mile of York river. We took a road leading to the right
but running parallel with and 1/2 mile from river. After moving
down this road some 500 yds, the loudest and most continued peels
of musketry greeted our ears. The gallant 1st – and brave 4th – with
the never-failing 18th Georgia were hard at work at the feast of
death. After having proceeded down this road – some 500 yds –
and being ignorant of the close proximity of the Yanks – we were
startled and surprised by a volley of minnies being poured into the
5th regt – wounding several & killing our commisary a brave &
noble man who was riding at the head of the regt.[17] Immediately
Col Archer ordered my company ("A") and Co "E" out on the left
flank – as skirmishers, and the regt drawn up in line of battle. I
myself was in a quandry. The old uniform of my comp. was a blue
shirt – & in this the primative days of the revolution the boys had a
mania for shooting at anything blue. Major Botts of the regt – came
to me and advised me to bid adieu to my old "Bayou City Guard"[18]
shirt – and for the sake of life, I set it free – and also bid adieu to a
Confederate Grey overcoat – which much impeded my movements.
After this sad surprise – we moved towards the river in line of battle
hearing all the time the loud musketry of the 1st & 4th hard at
work. After having marched some 600 yards – we halted and formed
line of battle at right angle with and 400 yds from the river facing
the battle. Directly the Yanks made their appearance – and with
right good will did open on them. We whiped them off – killing
some 50[19] – by this time we heard a deafening yell – which we recognized as coming from Texas – we immediately moved forward
to the scene of action – and found the 1st & 4th Texas and 18th

Georgia – charging & driving them. We joined our left to their right and drove them towards their gun boats – when in a few hundred yds of the river, their gun boats opened on us with grape shot – shell – and canister – Genl Hood ordered us to lay down. It was now about 11 A.M. – We remained in this position until 3 P.M. awaiting a new advance, but they never came. There had Franklin – with his 25,000 men been badly whiped by 7,000 determined Rebels[20] – in fact by 3,500 for Whiting's Brigade was not called into action. "Whiting's Brigade" was anxious to come in and join us, but that Genl told them in his blunt, offhand way – "never mind, them darn Texans will eat 'em all up." Genl Hood was everywhere that danger called. The 1st Texas bore the brunt of battle. The loss of our Brigade as many as I could learn numbered about 45 to 50.[21] This was our maiden fight and nobly did we sustain the reputation of our State. My emotions on going into battle – admit not of explanation – if reader you have never been where death reigned on the field of battle – you can not know what feelings move the heart. The 5th Texas was not heavily injured. The "Hampton Legion" of South Carolina under Col. Wade Hampton[22] bore a river port in this fight. At 3 P.M. we returned to our night camp – and until a late hour at night – a lively chat was kept up all over camp – each one giving in "his experiences" as for my part, my "prelims" were not the best. I had thrown away my coat and shirt in order to double-quick and now I was cold – in double-quicking after the Yanks my haversack string broke – and now I was minus my "two ears of corn," and for first time contrasted the comforts of home with my present situation. Thankful to my God for his protection – hungry, tired & sleepy – I lay down on my blanket about 11 P.M. Hardly had the delightful and restoring sensations of sleep fallen upon us – when the "long roll" sounded and by 2 A.M. we were under arms. Soon after laying down that night all our trains had left – and as we learnt afterwards – Johnston's veterans from "Williamsburg Field" – had passed by on the road for Richmond. We had saved our army and now we must save ourselves and if we had waited for a day we would have been captured. Well – yea very well, do I remember the 2 A.M. – 8th May. Never having been exposed or suffered fatigue – the march of the preceding days – the weting which I had got was now discovering itself upon me by

way of a chill and cramps. I was so sick, that I could hardly move –
but all our ambulances had left – and I must either be *captured* or
make an effort. We started off at a double quick – and in an hour –
I was all right again – by virtue of the exercise. Had the Yanks known
of our retrograde movement they could have injured us much. *Strict*
silence was the order from Gen. Hood, and for 10 miles, not a
voice above a whisper was heard, for every moment we expected to
be fired into by a Yankee ambush party to show the true state of
affairs. I copy from Chaplin Davis's (4th Texas) work on Hood's
Brigade,

> "What a hearty laugh a man could have had, had be been in a
> position to observe both armies that night. *Ours* moving swiftly
> and stealthily along, casting many and anxious glances to the rear
> fearing to discover the head of a pursueing column. *Theirs* dig-
> ging, toiling, and sweating, preparing to receive vigorous on-
> slaught which they knew the Rebels would make at daylight."[23]

We, once more were the rear guard of the Virginia Army. We
marched on hurriedly the remainder of the night, and soon after
day, we came upon "Barksdales (Mip) Brigade"[24] – we continued
the march – at an ordinary pace – all necessity for speed having
passed away. We continued on the road until 3 P.M. (May 8) when a
cluster of houses – a court house, jail – indicated that we were approaching a village – with colors flying and drums beating – we
passed through village, which was "New Kent Court House." Directly beyond the courthouse – in an open field we saw Confederate troops – who were to rest there that night and bring up the rear
next day. We marched on some four miles beyond – and struck
camp – and a happy moment it was too for four days we had been
on a forced march – in the worst of weather and on the worst of
roads – living on nothing – you might say – had fought a battle and
been victorious – and allowed but a few hours rest after the fight.
We had been marched hurriedly on and now we had a prospect of
a good nights rest and a good and abundant meal. The major part
of the army was on its way to Richmond and doubtless near there
– our halt here was also to check the enemy if they came on and
give the advancing portion of the Confederate Army time to form

around Richmond. Abundant rations of bacon & flour were issued us and having cooked our suppers – placed pickets on the branch roads to prevent a surprise – we returned to our "virtuous couches." For one who had hardly ever seen cooking done – I took to it finely – except in making my dough. I never could get it to stick together and at first I invariably made my biscuits so hard that they defied mastication.

Next morning (May 9th) we were up by . . . we rested on our arms until 2 P.M. – when the "long roll" beat – as yet the Yanks had not made their appearance. By half past 2 P.M. we took up the line of march for Richmond. Soon after starting a heavy rain began to pour down – and now indeed began the "tug of war." By dark – with the present and preceeding rain, the road became almost impassible and by 7 P.M. we could distinguish nothing five feet before us – so impenatrible was the darkness – but necesity compelled us on – and we thwarted the storm. We continued the march until 3 A.M. – passing over broken down and deserted wagons, mules and played out soldiers. Despite the hardship of the march – many ludicrous things occured. "Kersplash" – could now and then be heard from ahead and behind. Then would follow a big laugh by many mouths and some fellows would cry out – "come here Love & I will pick you up" – my humble self – rolled into a big ditch of mud & water – and was congratulating myself that my eyes were safe. By 3 A.M. – we came upon what is known as "confusion, confounded." Troops were huddled together, wagons tangled – with a hundred voices hollering and cursing their wearied mule teams. This proved to be "Chickahomany Bridge" over the Chickahomany River – a stream which from the scenes transpiring in its vacinity is known to history and to "Song."[25]

Then hast we marched since 3 P.M. to 3 A.M. – 12 hours – and had made but 6 miles – I again quote from Parson Davis's

"Here we found several Genl. all exhorting us to '*close up*' and for God's sake to hurry up and cross the bridge"[26]

– this was done as soon as the road way cleared. After crossing "Chickahomany Bridge" – we moved on and went into camp. By 5 A.M. the rear guard, had crossed the bridge, and the pioneers went to work – and soon *that* bridge was among the things that were. We went into camp by 4 A.M., built fires, hung our saturated clothes out to dry – received a pint cup full of flour 1/4 lb. of bacon for our next days rations. We were as much worn out men as you could find – but nature demanded sustenance, and soon the frying pan and skillet were performing their offices. As for myself I concluded to feast nature on a few "flap jacks." So borrowing a frying pan – I fried out my bacon – mixed my grease – a little water and my flour together – and the result of a days rations was 4 "flap jacks" and 2 specks of bacon. I immediately hid my bacon and three flap jacks – and taking the remaining one – I deposited it in my haversack for next days sustenance. We lay in camp until 11 A.M. next day – and then took up the line of march for Richmond. By 5 P.M. we found ourselves in 6 miles of Richmond near the "nine mile road" – and went into camp in a grove – near which lay some 40 cords of wood – and in 10 minutes not a stick was left – so soon as the companies had taken their camp ground. A rush was made for the wood – and each fellow busied himself – obtaining wood for *his* "mess." That night ample rations were issued – and we feasted merily on "flap jack" & "slush"[27] – two army dishes – which admit of no discription. At 9 A.M. (May 11th) we obeyed the "long roll" & started on the march and by 2 P.M. we were in camp at "Pine Island" – a beautiful pine grove on the Richmond & York River RR – and two miles from Richmond – with a view commanding the whole city.

Thus was the retreat from Yorktown performed one of the most brilliant military movements on record. Genl. Johnston naturaly retreated without any loss – but fought & won two battles – "Williamsburg" & "West Point" – captured many prisoners – and many arms.[28] He was persued by a Yankee army three times his number, well disciplined and equiped.[29] I am by no means an admirer of "Old Joe" – but I believe in the adage "Render unto Ceaser, that which is Ceasers due." For this brilliant move Genl Johnston deserves the gratitude of his country. For this *single* move – he deserves the eulogies of his countrymen – as a move – brilliant in the extreme.

Chapter 3

SEVEN PINES

$\mathscr{W}$e were informed that this camp would for awhile be permanent and by general consent it was designed as "Camp Pine Island." Everything assumed the appearance of a little village. Tents and "brush houses" were soon raised. Abundance of rations such as bacon, rice, beans, flour & meal were issued. Men were busy in cleaning their guns – attending drills, inspection and parades – washing and "*lousing.*" The last named employment became a science and a soldiers merit is based upon the number of "war bugs" he carries, and his skill in capturing. Now and then you could see a fellow suddenly run his hand into his clothes – scratch – withdraw it – and cry out – "Louse or no louse" (at the same time having his thumb and forefinger closed) and numerous were the responses from his immediate comrades. During the day a heavy guard was posted – and at night pickets were stationed out "countersign" *Baltimore.* This was the first place where I was on post.

The 1st Texas being a 12 month regiment here swore in "for this War" and elected officers – Col Raines[1] – their old col. who distinguished himself at "West Point" was selected Col. Capt. Work[2] – Lt Col – Lt Matt Dale[3] – Major. The officers of my company were all young and popular men – in fact – they were our associates when at home. D. C. Farmer[4] a young Kentuckian by birth – was Capt – John Hale[5] a Virginian by birth was 1st Lieut. James Clute a New Yorker by birth – but as noble – brave and generous soul as ever lived – was 2nd Lt. B. P. Fuller [6] a native Texan was our 3rd Lt. At this camp I applied for leave of absence to visit Richmond a day – and it was granted. In all my visits to & sojourns in towns & city . . . my money was usually laid out in segars – nick nacks and finery – but now on leaving Richmond on my return to camp – I was sweating under a side of bacon – 10lbs of coffee and sugar – soda – and numerous substantials – all welcome to my "Mess." Here I with several others found a "*Mess*" which lasted until nearly all of us had been laid on the shelf, which was nearly two years compounded of Thos. W. Fitzgerald[7] one of the bravest of the Regt. – Owen O'Malley,[8] a brave and gallant soldier – W. P. Morell[9] – a clever, witty and ingenious fellow – and my humble self – we ranked "*No 14*" and all of us lived greatly and peacefully together.

We remained in this camp – living well for soldiers and doing nothing until the evening of May 29th when we were aroused from our haunts and pursuits by the "long roll" – which is always ominous of active moves – and activity is generally the precursor of battle. Soon tents disappeared – cooking utensils were in the wagons, canteens and haversacks filled and all ready for the "*unknown move.*" By 5 P.M. we took up the line of march and had hardly started before the rain began to fall and by 7 P.M. we were in the dark and mud a repetition of our "Chickahomany March" – we marched on circling around Richmond – and on the "Hanover Court House road" – just before daylight we halted – and wet – muddy and tired we lay down and went to sleep. By 9 A.M. – (30th) we were woke up – kindling our fires – broiling a slice of bacon and eating a biscuit was soon accomplished. We had made but five miles during the previous night march. We now retraced our steps and after marching 3 miles – were halted in a grove – on the Virginia Central RR – within two miles of Richmond and by 4 P.M. – we were around our campfire – the rain coming down in showers. That night I was detached "on guard" – a most gloomy prospect. After dark numbers of the boys "ran the Blockade" – by going into Richmond without passes. I took my place on post until 11 P.M. I walked my post the cold wind and rain beating against and through my clothes. When relieved I returned to the Guard House and lay down to rest. Having nothing but one blanket to lay on and cover with too – I carefully groped my way in the dark – seeking for a dry place on which to lay. Failing in this I lay two poles lengthwise and deposited my wearied limbs upon them. At daylight when woke up to go on post – I was lying in a mud puddle and so tired was I that I enjoyed my sleep in a puddle of mud as if I had been upon a feather bed.

On the night of May 25th Genl McLelland had crossed over to the Richmond side of the "Chickahomany River" a large force of Yanks. Two corps – numbering 20 odd thousand[10] – they were commanded by Major Genl Casy.[11] They had up to this time been fortifying in the vacinity of the nine mile road some 15 miles below Richmond towards the Peninsula – and protected their front by felled trees – abbatis and sharpened stakes – besides a very boggy swamp protecting their front. Their lines were mounted with very heavy canon – and in all appearances their position was impregnable.

Since their crossing over the heavy rains had so swolen and increased the waters of the "Chickahomany" that our Genl Johnston supposed them to be isolated and cut off from all communication with Genl McLelland and the main army – and consequently he determined to attack them – and if possible capture the whole force with the many and valuable supplies which they possessed.

The "Battle-of-Seven Pines." *30th May & June 1*

In view of this attack – Genl J. had concentrated some five or six brigades under Major Genl. James Longstreet[12] in a position near the enemy on the night of May 30th.[13] I will now return to "Whitings Sub Division" – which I left in camp near Richmond – which camp the boys on account of the stormy night passed there, dubed "Camp Thunder and Lightning."

After being relieved from off post in the morning I returned to the company expecting the "Mess" would have me a warm breakfast – when I was informed by them during the night – the wind had blown down our tent and our bacon with it – and it had floated off. As for the flour – it was lying near by in a mud puddle. Consoling myself the best way I could, I returned with disapointment and a hungry stomach – and busyed myself in drying my clothes. By 9 A.M. the "long roll" beat, and at a double quick we started for Richmond – but on nearing it – we passed around – and took the road leading towards the Chickahomany Swamp. Hardly had we passed around R – before the boom of canon and roar of musketry broke upon the still air – "going to have a frolic." "Now we can dance a war dance boys" and many such exclamations were utered by our Texas boys. We moved on down until opposite and about 4 miles from the fight. It was now about 1 P.M. We halted in the road and stacked arms. Soon after halting we were joined by the boys, who the previous evening had run the blockade into Richmond. Awful indeed was our present suspense – lying on our arms, and expecting every moment to be ordered to the scene of death. The fight went briskly on. Now and then some stragler from his post would come by – and represent our army as whiped, but a stragler who leaves his post in the hour of battle speaks not the truth. Men with flesh wounds – come bloody, limping by – litters occupied with badly wounded come thickly from the bloody field. Ambulances by the dozens loaded with dead and dying went tearing by to Richmond. Ah!

Imagine *our* feeling – who were expecting every moment the order, "Forward" – and, it *did* come. By 4 P.M. Genl. Hood rode up. "Attention" "Soldiers – you will pile up your blankets and haversacks, and each company leave a guard with its own effects" "Load at will, but do not cap *yet*." With a mental prayer to my God – a thought of home and the loved ones, I loaded and prepared for action. We marched across fields – through woods – in the direction of the battle. In half hour – we came across deserted works – dead and dying of both sides lay thick around. Near by were Yankee tents – piled with all that could please the taste or tempt a "Beau Brummel." This was in the beginning of the war – and men fought not to plunder. Not a man left his place to sieze the deserted Yankee "notions." Proceeding a few hundred yards farther – a volley of "minnies" and a Yankee shell came flying along. We plunged into a swamp – waist deep – and for six hundred yards, holding our guns and ammunition up – we waded on – and after going these 600 yds – we emerged upon a cleared ground. Then the order came "*Cap.*" This cleared ground had been a thick pine forest. The Yanks had occupied it – cut down all the trees – dug a line of works and fortified heavily with canon and . . . long and bloody was the contest before we carried it. The . . . were . . . over and tangled up. What sight flashed upon our view – it defies description.

This position had been charged and carried by the 4th & 5th Florida Volunteers.[14] The Floridians were ordered forward – and like brave and gallant men, moved forward – determined to die or conquer – but how dearly did the triumph cost them? How bloody was their wake. The gallant Floridians lay dead and dying on every side, here one in the agony of death, imploring the passerby to ease his thirst with a cool draught of water, here lies another, immersed in a pond of water, with his hands even in death in the act of aiming and firing. There another, lying dead across a fallen tree, which he was in the act of crossing, when the fatal missle came. There a group lie huddled together, laid low by the bursting of a shell – and from all in whom life was yet left – rose that well known cry "water – water, for Gods sake – give me a drink." We could not now alleviate their agony – our work of death was before us. Such a scene I never beheld, but Florida can well point with pride to the many green hillocks on the battle field of "Seven Pines" attesting its devotion to and bravery in the cause. We proceeded on and soon came up with the fleeing Yanks. The cheers of our boys – clearly told that the field was won. We joined in the pursuit and were under fire but a few moments. Night was upon us. We were in a dense swamp and our regt. (5th) was cut off from the Brigade. It was now so dark, that nothing could be distinguished – and in our charge we followed the Yanks – ignorant of our bearing. Not far from us – could be heard the tramp of the Yanks retreating – the voices of their officers giving command. We were in a dilemma. Our Col. (Archer) sent out several of the boys to find the command, but they returned having done nothing. Col. A, despite the Yanks cried out in a loud voice for Genl. Hood – and a courier heard him, who had been sent to hunt us – and in a few moments he led us to the Brigade, whom we found camped on the "Nine Mile R." Wet and wearried – without the least covering we lay down to rest and it was now very cold. We learnt that night that Genl Johnston had been seriously but not dangerously wounded – also that Genl. Hatton[15] of Tenn. Brigade was killed. Genl. Pettigrew[16] of North Carolina badly wounded and captured. We had been successful in every charge but had lost heavily. Soon after laying down – some one reported that a Yankee camp – deserted in the morning, was near at hand. A great many of the boys – with pine torches broke for the camp – among the number my messmate Owen Omally and fortunate for me for I had been asleep but a few moments on the wet ground, when I was siezed with severe cramps – which seemed nearly killing me – and on geting up – and looking around I discovered someone approaching – who proved to be Omally. He was loaded down with blankets and "Yankee Notions." He reported the camp was well stored. Dinners were prepared – brandy and . . . all ready – which the Yankee officers were ready to devour – when our troublesome Confederates made them leave in quick time. While the boys were plundering – 50 Massachusetts Volunteers – came running up to obtain some of their deserted property – but on seeing *their* camp occupied by Rebs they took to their heels.[17] After refreshing the inner man on captured eatables – I rolled my captured blanket around me and sank into a sweet slumber. Next day Omally shared his captured envelopes – letter paper, with their fancy designs, and a pile of love letters, which the Yanks didn't have gallantry to defend. Ah Yankee Maidens – you have but poor representatives at the seat of war!

Next morning (June 1st) we were under arms. The 5th Texas occupied the ground to the right of the Rail Road,[18] the 1st, 4th Txs and 18th Ga. the ground to the left. During the night Genl McLelland had reinforced Genl Casey with two corps – by running a pontoon bridge over the Chickahomany and intended to charge and if possible retake his last position – . . . and . . . – he mistook his foe. Here [is] where Genl J. was wrong. He did not believe that McLelland could reinforce on our side of the RR – the timber had been felled. We moved forward a few hundred yards and formed a line parallel to the road – and had halted – stacked our arms – and were in the act of ascending the "railroad" bank to take a surrounding view – when a heavy fire of musketry was opened upon us. Col Archer formed us in line and ordered us to fall back to a rail fence some 200 yds distant – which we did in fine order – though under heavy fire.

We occupied this position during the day – under fire from a Yankee battery all the time. The Yanks charged and charged again, but our boys stood firm, sending many hundreds to their long home. By 3 P.M. the Yanks drew off in disgust – whiped at every point. That night they recrossed the Chickahomany. Thus was fought and won the battle of "Seven Pines" a bloody battle indeed. "Hoods Brigade lost but few."[19]

The Confederate loss in this battle was not over 4500 – all told.[20] The Yanks lost at least 10,000, prisoners included – besides many arms – canon – commisary and ordinance stores.[21]

Genl. R. E. Lee[22] now took command of the "Army of Northern Virginia."

Chapter 4

JOINING JACKSON

*G*enl. Johnston being wounded – the command devolved upon *Genl. Robt E Lee* – by appointment – and the Confederate Army in this portion of the Confederacy was by Genl Orders – designated as "Army of Northern Virginia" – Concerning our noble, brave, generous and beloved commander – words fail to express how highly he is prized – nor could words from me indicate clearly his beautiful traits, for he is known to the world – his acts whether in his personal intercourse with his soldiers on the field of battle – whether in his communication with the enemy – stand for themselves – each wanting in itself to render his name immortal. The world may admire the citizens of the "ex Confederate States," may render homage and associate his name with all that is *good* – but it is for the soldiers of the "*Virginia* Army" – to love their true and gallant leader – with a love – which none other than *Lee* could inspire. I know of no subject – no theme which is so beautiful to write upon as the *character* of Genl *R. E. Lee,* a character but seldom seen

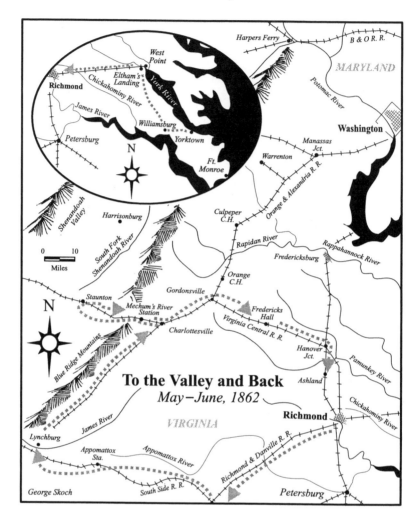

in times like the past. He was not alone – a military man – The Captain of the age – but he was a *christian* – in the broadest sense of the word, gentle – kind-generous – brave – and worthy of all praise, which grateful countrymen – or admiring nations can give. During the past winter – troops had been organizing all over the south – and now they were reinforcing the different armies of the Confederacy. Many new regiments joined us from time to time – and our army numbered – so far as I could learn, when Genl. Lee took command, near 40,000.[1] Troops on their first arrival – formed camps of instruction – and were for a while kept busy – becoming disciplined – and were not placed immediately at the front. The battle of "Seven Pines" was now over – & we were at liberty – (as *we* thought) to return to Camp and live until another battle – an easy life – a *mistake!*

On the evening of June 1st, as soon as the Yanks had withdrawn, and the battle ended – we formed line and marched back to the place where we had left our baggage under guard and selecting a camp on the "James City road" four miles from Richmond, we retired to our blankets – and in the society of our pipes – we cogitated on dangers surmounted. Many though of our fellow Confederates were sleeping their last long sleep – who but a few days before – were fair and happy.

On the morning of June 2nd we marched towards the Chickahomany Swamp where our outpost lines and advanced pickets were. We took the road – known as the White House road – and having advanced some 6 miles from Richmond, we came across an Alabama Brigade who were on picket.[2] We relieved them and they returned to the rear to rest. It had been raining several days – and the ground was covered with water. Whiskey – hard tack and salt pork were issued to us here. At night we were compelled to make our beds on the wet ground – and on awaking – were damp and chilled to the skin. It was here that I was on picket – in a slow drizly rain – and when at 2 P.M. – the relief guard came round to place on fresh pickets, I found my right hand picket – sound asleep – the penalty of which is death – but our kind hearted sergent did not report him. In this mud hole – we remained a couple of weeks or so, guarding the lines – being on three days – and going to the rear and resting two – then on again. Picket duty is certainly very hard and wearing. On post, you are exposed to the fire of the Yankee Picket – in all kinds of weather. At this very place – I stood post, in a heavy rain – shaking all the time with a hard chill yet I did not give up.

For awhile I will leave the Brigade in their duty of guarding our lines near Richmond – and briefly refer to the brilliant career of "Stonewall" Jackson[3] – not to point its glory or to follow his brilliant footsteps – for this task belongs to an abler pen than mine – but because a relation exists between his moves (rather a consequence) and "Whitings' Sub Div." Allow me to say before beginning this subject – that we (5th Txs) had lost our brave and well loved Col – J J Archer – while on picket duty a few days after "Seven Pines" – he went into Richmond and returning to the regt the next day – we were formed in line by our Lt Col J B Robertson – when Col Archer said – "My comrades – I have been honored by the President with a commission as Brig Genl of a Tenn Brigade. I love you – always shall – our associations have ever been pleasant – Soldiers – farewell." With that he rode off in a gallop. The boys began to cheer. He halted – turned around – and every one could see the tears pouring down his eyes. He could not speak. He waved a military salute and rode off. Archer – who is now no more – was brave – generous and kind and a strict disciplinarian. The men loved him – Lt Col Robertson became Col – Maj Brown Botts Lt Col – and J C Upton[4] of Co "B" – a daredevil – open hearted and brave Texan – became Major.

"Stonewall Jackson" – with two divisions of the Army, his own – and Ewell's[5] had moved into the Shenandoah Valley some two months previous, in order to protect that country and to defeat Genl Banks[6] who was commdg the Yanks in the Valley. A few weeks before the battle of "Seven Pines" Banks – Milroy,[7] Shields[8] and Fremont[9] – each commanded an army in the valley for the purpose of exterminating "Stonewall Jackson."

"Stonewall" began his campaign most actively and it was here that he gained his most brilliant reputation – as a soldier. Knowing that should the different Yankee Genls combine, he determined to whip them in detail if possible since they were each occupying distant points from one another. Now began some of the most brilliant moves on record. Jackson – before Banks knew of his proximity, pitched into him – whiped & routed his army, capturing stores & army munitions.[10] Hardly giving his battle veterans time to rest – he moved with the greatest . . . , over mountains – across rivers and valleys – and in the Battle of Winchester – and several other hard fought fields – not only whiped Fremont, Banks & Co. – but drove them from the Valley – and now – was occupying a position some 30 miles above Staunton. McLelland was gradually approaching Richmond, and had by this time (June 11) occupied all the Rail Roads (3)[11] heading from Richmond – on the North James – he was as near as 4 1/2 miles from the city at some points, and it behoved us to retard his "spade and pick" advances – by the rifle.

Every step he fortified and was day by day diging his way into the "Confederate capital."

After the battle of "Seven Pines," as I observed before, our subdivision under Brig Genl Whiting had been doing hard and dangerous duty on the picket line.[12] On the evening of 9th we were relieved from the front and marched to camp near Richmond (3 miles). On the evening of the 10th June, 3 days rations were issued, ordered to be cooked and preparations be made to march next morning. "Where are we going?" "What are we going to do?" and a hundred and one questions escaped our lips – on the reception of these orders.

On the morning of the 11th the Texas Brigade and Col Louis' Alabama Brigade[13] – (the component of the "sub Div") under Brig Genl Whiting – marched into Richmond – and found cars awaiting us which would transport the command to Lynchburg. The boys having imbibed pretty freely in their brief stay at Richmond became very gay – and from Richmond to Lynchburg, were singing songs – and cheering the pretty girls at the way stations – who came to bid us god speed. We arrived at Lynchburg that evening, and camped in the suberbs of the city – where we remained some 4 days. Lieut Clute was the only officer present in the company – all the others being absent sick. It was now generally understood that we were bound for the Shenandoah Valley to join "Stonewall" and as we thought, invade "Maryland My Maryland." We were here issued shoes and clothing, though not enough to suffice, for up to this time, soldiers had mostly been provided for by friends and kindered at home. Here our Lieut Col – Brown Botts left us and went into hospital. No tears were shed – for he was neither honored or loved. After being here some four days – we took the cars for Charlottsville, where we arrived in six hours, leaving the cars we marched up to the famed "University of Virginia" and were quartered on the campus – so Hood's Brigade can always say that they have been *through* the "University of Virginia." On arriving in C. I was nearly famished and some two or three of us charged a "dutch shoe makers" shop and with Texas eloquence persuaded on him and his "frow" to give us a morsel. "Vell" said our Teutonic host "Yu bese from Dexas. Vell since Ize got brudder vat goes dare – so much long time agoes, I gives you some dinner." The old shoe maker placed before each of us a big pickle, a chicken leg and a biscuit – and I then thought that I had never set down to such a meal in my life. Paying him a dollar a piece – we took a grateful farewell – and the boys in camp hearing of it – came by the dozens – but our German friend would feed no more on account of "his brudder in Dexas." On my way to the University who should I meet but my messmate O'Mally, who had been on the "hunt" – some two hours and was rewarded with a "stewed chicken" – and was now hunting the mess. I helped him devour it also. On arriving at the company I was detailed on guard and stationed at one of the University gates – with strict orders to let no one pass in or out, and I was happy in the position, for soon the Ladies came promenading down to see the "Texicans" – and I saw the "Charlottsville Beauties." At Lynchburg we were joined by Genl Lawton[14] with his brigade of Georgians – Lawton afterwards left the field to become "Quartermaster Genl." Remaining at Charlottsville but one day we took the cars for Staunton – situated . . . and the "Blue Ridge Mts" – and at the end of the Shenandoah Valley. Arriving at Staunton in a few hrs we left the cars and marched through the city to a grove just beyond several delightful springs adjacent – and went into camp. All along on our trip from Richmond we had for soldiers feasted finely. Strawberries – fruits of all kinds, butter and milk – big loaves of light bread – flowed upon us. We had been in camp but an hour or two, when in the distance could we discern colums of marching troops – and the cry *"Stonewall"* rose from every voice and soon the hero of many bloody but victorious fields with his old and gallant veterans marched into town and camped near by.

It was on the evening of June 21st 62 that we arrived at Staunton – as soon as we had went into camp, I was placed on guard and consequently had but little time to take a "birds eye view" of the beautiful and mountainous city of Staunton. "Here" our mess feasted high – for which we were indebted to our messmate Mr Morrell. "Merchant Tailor" At dawn on the morn of the 22nd, the "Long Roll" sounded – and soon, tents in wagons, blankets and haversacks and rifle on our shoulders, we were ready to go wheresoever the "powers that were" desired. By 7 A.M. we bid adieu to the "fair women" and "brave stay at homes" of Staunton. Taking a road that ran parallel for 5 miles with the Virginia Central RR leading to Charlotsville via Beachams Station – 20 miles from Staunton. Thus we were on the back track. "What's up?" cried the boys. "Whats up?" answered echo. After marching a half hour, several trains sped by, having on board – portions of "Stonewalls" corps – as if by intuition we at once knew "a rear movement on Little Mac and Richmond." We marched on until 11 A.M. on a hard solid turnpike – lined on each side by beautiful clear springs. By 11 A.M. we struck the base of the "Blue Ridge" Mountains – and with slow and measured step we began the ascent. In an hour we were on their tops, and what a lovely sight fell upon our gaze. What a contrast did the busy homebound men of the farms – which were visable in all directions, present to the business to which we Confederates were devoting ourselves.

In the direction of Charlotsville could be seen portions of Jackson's Corps marching on to the coming carnage. We descended the mountains and by 2 P.M. were at Beachams Station, where we found Genl Whiting with trains awaiting us. Soon we were on the cars, and went puffing away, towards Charlotsville. On reaching C we did not stop – but went whizing through the city, mid cheers of the "fair sex." Soon after leaving C, we came across other portions of Jacksons Corps – and then we *knew* our *destination* was not "My Maryland" but McLelland's rear.

By 4 P.M. we had reached "Frederick Halls" station on the "Virginia Central" distant from Richmond some 70 miles. This was as far as we could go – for the Yanks held the road some ten miles below – cuting us off from Richmond. We were soon disembarked from the "Iron Horse's train" & marched some half mile from Fredericks Hall to an oak woods and went into camp. We were now a part of "Stonewall Jacksons" corps. The old *hero* was already here and had established his "Hd Qurt."

Next day was Sunday, and at the dress parade and inspection early in the morning – genl orders were read from Genl Jackson – notofying the troops that devine service would be held at the church near Frederick Hall, and all of his soldiers were permitted. Yea, he invited them to attend "all duties not absolutely necessary" were for the day dispensed with. Many of the boys went, and among the most pious, attentive and humble among the congregation was the illustrious chief – so those of the company who attended told – for I, sinner that I was did not go. During the day the most of Jacksons "Old Valley Army" arrived and went into camp. We were now 20,000 strong[15] an army nearly as large as the *whole* Virginia Army under Johnston at the retreat from the Peninsula. Here my messmate "Morrell, Merchant Tailor" visited a Lady – who boasted of a "Tailor husband" and our friend Mr. Morrell worked upon her sympathies to the amount of some butter, eggs and a few dilicacies by reason of the strange co-incidence of his being and her husbands being *"Tailors"* sharp fellow that Morrell – as the sequel will prove. "Our Mess" was honored by a present of boquets and "nick nacks" from several beautiful Virginia girls – by reason of the handsome Mr. Dimsy Walker[16] of said mess . . ."Two days rations" were issued and ordered to be cooked up – and also ordered to be ready to march at daylight the next morning (24). By day we were up by 6 A.M. – on the march – taking the road that leads to Hanover Junction, some 30 miles off. We marched on during the day, meeting no sign of an enemy, and nothing of importance transpiring. By night we had made 20 miles. Wearied with the hard days march we soon sank to sweet slumber, dreaming of home and the "gal I left behind me."

Next morning (25) early, we were again ploding onward towards the "Cerulian Bellies." At this stage of the game my dilapidated shoes refused to cling to my wearied feet longer. So with gratitude for the good they had done – I bid adieu and stumbled on barefooted over stones & clods – and a sweet time I did have. On near Hanover Junction, we left it to our left – and took the road for Ashland – a beautiful country town – suited by Rich Virginia planters as a summer retreat – and distant some 30 miles from Richmond. Our brigade being in the advance column we for the first time beheld the Yanks – retreating from Ashland as our cavalry occupied it. They showed no fight – for which we felt grateful – as we were weared out.

Chapter 5

THE SEVEN DAYS BATTLES

$\mathcal{W}$e went into camp near Ashland and were soon busy cooking up 3 days rations. Rumors were soon afloat in camp that a body of Texans would join us in the morning – among them the 2nd Texas – and we were anxious to welcome our Texas comrades.[1] A long order was received directing company commanders to report to Brigade Hd Qurts. After Lieut Clute returned from Genl. Hood's Qurts – he called the company around him and said "Boys, we march in the morning early – on line for the Yankee rear – a bloody battle is to be fought. Genl Jackson directs that soldiers keep their places, keep up & don't straggle. Already McLelland is nonplussed – and by enduring bravely the coming dangers & hardships – our Capital will be free and victory on our banners." A hearty cheer was raised which spoke the determination of all to "conquer or die."

McLelland with his hordes had now to *fight,* or *ingloriously* re-treat – and the last he could not do. The Yankee nation and officials would not consent, even did Little Mc. desire.

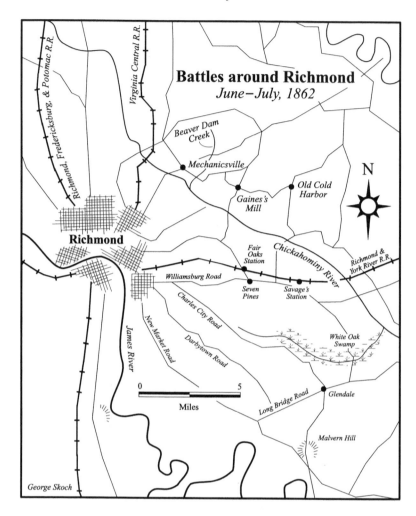

His rear was not only threatened, but the columns of Stonewall from their victorious valley campaign were coming down on him like an avalache. He *must* fight even if defeat were certain. His army was numerous – supplied with all (except moral courage) that could give victory. Our army was small – badly supplied – but made up in courage – determination and conscienceness of their right, for all deficiencies otherwise. Jackson had in his rear movement as I said before, some 20,000 men. Genl Lee – confronting McLelland and had some 25,000, perhaps 30,000[2] – enough at all events – to drive the Hessians from our Capital.

"Battles around Richmond"

Were a minute history of these battles (which are now familliarly known as "Seven Day Fight") written, the topography, various incidents etc. written, it would occupy a large column – and though a participant in this 7 day fight, neither my reccollection or discriptive powers justify me in treating of them otherwise than in a very brief manner, confining myself to the part that my brigade and more particularly my regt. acted – for my position as a humble private, with the duty of encountering the foe immediately in my front, is reason enough of my ignorance of other positions of the field. "Whitings Sub Div" – was *conspicuously* engaged in the battles of "Gaines Mill" and "Malvern Hill" of that fight, hense I shall dwell upon them more extensively. "Stonewalls" command consisted of Ewells Div. and his own Div. under A. P. Hill,[3] "Whitings Sub Div." and two Brigades of cavalry – in all some 20,000 men.

We left Jacksons army camped near Ashland – on the evening of June 25th. On the morning of June 26th, we were awakened from our slumber by the "long roll." By 3 A.M. – 4 A.M. it found us on the move. We took a Richmond road, via Mechanicsville. By 8 A.M. we could hear firing ahead which was our cavalry driving back the Yankee mounted men. By 11 A.M. Ewells Div formed in line of battle – and "Hoods Brigade" was stationed out on the flank – A. P. Hills Div – followed as a reserve. At 1 P.M. – marching slowly on – through fields, down roads and among the woods – we began to hear the skirmishers rifle – and directly our Brigade was stoped, to clear the road, and hastily reconstruct a burned bridge. All these things denote our proximity to McLellands main body. Soon the firing increased – and in an hour – it was a deafening roar. Musketry and artillery – soon Yankee prisoners – wounded Confederates and the hurrying to & fro denoted that the battle of "Mechanicsville" was in progress. Mechanicsville is a little burg, some 15 miles from Richmond – and was the extreme right flank of the Yankee Army. McLelland had fortified heavily, had heavy ordnance – and an abundance of supplies, *not,* however calculating on this rear movement of ours.

Ewell with his Div. struck their works and they desperately resisted him. Soon A. P. Hills Div. joined him – and as they started on the charge, a shout ascended which was deafening. They charged – despite the flying of rifle balls, the bursting of shells and canister carrying away hundreds of lives, and by 3 P.M. the Confederate banner waved over Mechanicsville. The enemy after being driven out of their works – still contested the day, but by 4 P.M. our boys had crushed their spirits and then began a hurried retreat, leaving everything they had, all kinds of arms and stores of commisary supplies. By 5 P.M. the battle was over and our arms victorious. We selected a beautiful place near a meadow and went into camp – and in a few moments J E B Stewart[4] – with his cavalry, just from his noted raid around McLelland's Army made their appearance – stationed a cavalry picket in our front, and moved forward to harrass the retreating foe. That night at 11 P.M. the *5th* Texas Regt – while sound asleep – all of a sudden jumped to their arms crying "The Yankee Cavalry is on us." It seems that a horse tread upon a fellows foot while asleep – and he cried cavalry.

The battle of "Mechanicsville" was ended and a victory to the Confederate Arms. "Whiting's Sub Div" was not engaged – protecting the flanks of Jacksons army during the entire day. Concerning our loss, I cannot speak with certainty and term it best, for the sake of truth, not to speak as "haphazard." Everything tended to show that McLelland would desperately dispute every inch of ground – and if victorious it would be at the cost of much blood. At daybreak on the morning of the *27th* June, the "long roll" sounded, and soon we were under arms, prepared for what might come. We took the line of march – following roads which ran parallel with McLellands line. McLellands right flank was now turned & concentrating on that flank a heavy force, he was prepared to resist, and if possible restore his lines. Communication was now established between Genl Lee and Genl Jackson. We continued on the march, still guarding Jacksons flank. By 8 A.M. fireing began – McLelland was now contesting the ground between Mechanicsville and Coal Harbor.[5] The fireing increased – growing "heavier and deadlier" than before. Ambulances were flying to and fro bearing off the dead and dying – gangs of Yankee prisoners came back under guard – "*on their way to Richmond.*" By 1 P.M. we were halted near a body of woods, being wearied and heated (as the day was excessively warm). During this halt 60 rounds of cartridges were

issued to each soldier.[6] The bugler of the *5th* Sandy by name stray-
ing off a piece into the woods, came across some 25 men of the
"Pensylvania Bucktail Regt" – all armed – with guns loaded, and
hid in the bushes.[7] The musical man demanded their surrender,
having nothing but his "*bugle*," they were inclined to laugh at him
and, when Sandy raising his bugle towards his mouth exclaimed "If
I just blow my bugle, de Texans who be just dar in edge of de woods,
vill all come runing here and vill kill all – 20 yus come vid me and
dey no hurtz you." They submitted and were soon among us, dis-
tributing their ammunition & caps to the boys. I myself got a lot
and used against them that very day. They (the Bucktails) were placed
under guard and sent to the rear. McLelland had now been driven
to Gaines Mill, the strongest position on his line – and where he
hoped to be able to administer a telling defeat. It was entrenched –
held by his best troops – mounted with many large and small cali-
bre canon – and on the result of the fight there depended his future.

"Gaines Mill" 27th June-1862

I will endeavor, in my homely way, to give some idea of the topography of this battlefield, at least of that position where "Whitings
Sub Div" engaged in bloody contest the "chosen bands" of Yankee
chivalry.

Gaines Mill is situated on a runing branch by which it is pro-
pelled. This branch runs some two miles in direction of James river
and as you leave the Mill – the banks on either side begin to ascend
– and in half mile of the mill they are very steep – and some 50 feet
deep – and near this position are large eminences which McLelland
had fortified. On the Richmond side of this run, beginning at and
runing some 400 yards back – and extending along the bank of the
branch – is a woodland. Trees had filled the side of the banks – but
had been cut down by the Yanks – and now formed an almost im-
passable barrier. The enemy had fortified the brow of the hill or
banks – on their side of this branch – and in their intrenchments
were thick as black birds. So to charge them – we would have to
descend our side of the hill – under fire and obstructed by felled
trees, would have to wade the branch, and then ascend their side of
the hill – and make our way over trees and sharpened stakes – and

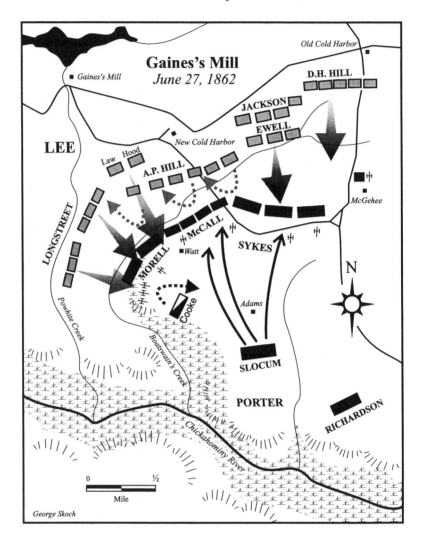

Gaines's Mill
June 27, 1862

George Skoch

under a murderous fire. The line defending this Gaines Mill position, was some mile and a half & many a noble soul would have to surrender life before we could drive them from their stronghold. Genl Lee with his devoted soldiers were equal to the task.

Maj Genl Longstreet opened the battle at this line – though a mile to the right of the Mill. Virginians[8] principally engaged the Yanks in their stronghold near the Mill.

Up to this hour (4 P.M.) the battle had been rageing – with an awful sacrifice of life on our side. *Our* troops had charged and charged again – carried the works at some points, but were on the whole – unsuccessful. At no point did the Yanks seem so defiant and immoveable as at Gaines Mill – no less than 3 fresh lines of battle had charged them and each time were hurled back, bleeding, maimed and thined.

As we (Whitings Sub Div) were marching along, protecting the flank – listening to the roar of bloody battle – and beholding the filled Ambulances as they hurried to the rear – with our maimed and dying boys, a staff officer from Genl. Jackson galloped up, and delivering his orders, we immediately moved by the left flank – towards the heavy firing. Leaving the main road we moved across an open field – and took our position in a lane parallel to the line of battle. Here we found the "Hampton Legion" of South Carolina, who were attached to the Brigade. Immediately – orders were given to load and cap. Line of battle was quickly formed—4th Txs on extreme right – next 18th Ga. 5th Texas in center – then 1st Txs, and the "Hampton Legion" on extreme left. *We were now ready for battle.* We moved out of the lane in battle array – into a little field – which intervened between us and a body of woods – at a double quick, we crossed this field and entered the woods, we found the woods filled with stragglers – and just ahead a few hundred yards – we could see the smoke of battle, and our boys hard at work – already the Yankee balls began to fly among us. The 4th line of battle had gone in, made a charge and been repulsed. With the gallant Hood at our head – we moved forward, a heavy fire, both from artillery and rifles being poured into us – we moved up to the brow of the hill, (before described) which confronted the Yankee breastworks on the opposite brow – The Virginians fell back. As soon as arriving at this hill, we were ordered to lay down, and commenced a brisk fire upon the enemy. Co. K of the 5th was detached as skirmishers – our brave Lt. Col. J. C. Upton – a Texas stock man, but as noble, brave and generous as ever lived, was walking up and down the regt – calling on us "My brave boys, give it to them" and then he would wave his saber over his head and give a yell. About this time, an officer dashed up and began in the following strain "Don't run my boys, give it to them – stand my men, for Gods sake stand – or the day is lost." Balls of all discription were flying like hail and now and then a groan would tell us of some brave comrade who was no more. As soon as this officer invoked us "For Gods sake stand," Col. Upton ran up to him and in an awful anger, cried out "Who in the hell and damnation are you?" "I am a staff officer of Genl. Ewells" – replied he. "Leave here, you damn coward, these are my men, these are Texans, and they *don't know* how to run – and sir, if you don't leave here immediately, I will teach you how to run." The officer hesitated not a moment – for he knew from Col. Upton, that he meant what he said. About this time the clarion voice of Genl. Hood was heard "*Attention*" and in a second every man was to his feet.

"*Fix Bayonets*" and in a second the bright steel points glistened along our line. The dead and dying lay thick around us. The declivity which we had to descend, was strewn with the bodies of those who had charged before us. "*Forward*" said old Hood, and with a leap and a yell, heard for miles around, we *pitched* down the bank, jumping over felled trees. Genl. Hood lead the 4th Texas (his old regt) Genl. Archer (our former Col.) was in reserve with his brigade, as soon as he heard our yell, remarked to his command "There go the Texans and my old regt, and they will sweep everything before them." Down the hill we went, yelling like mad men, with men falling at every step – we reached the ravine and plunged in, and in drawing my foot from the mud and water, I lost a shoe – but *now* was no time to tarry. Up the hill we started, climbing over felled trees and sharpened stakes – toiling and tuging away, whooping and yelling, comrades falling on all sides we steadily but rapidly advanced upon our foe – who imagined that we would be driven back like the four preceeding lines of battle. But the Lone Star flag[9] – which had been upon the field of "San Jacinto" cheered us on and we moved into the very mouth of their belching canon. They allowed us to get in ten paces of them, when seeing that we were determined to *do* or *die,* they broke like cowardly dogs and left their works to us. With a yell we leaped into them, waved our banner oer their fortifications, and started in pursuit. After leaving their works – we emerged into a field – which extended for miles. In all directions could be seen the fleeing Yanks – and as we started in pursuit – the regimental flags of the whole Brigade were right and left. Now their numerous batteries from the hills began to play upon us and as we were charging on a battery the gallant George Onderdonk[10] – color sergt of my Regt – fell wounded – and as he fell, he raised the flag on high, and Tom Watson[11] of Co. "E" snatching it bore it on. In a few moments it was waving over the Yankee battery. The enemy were fleeing in all directions – and for a few moments we sat down to regain strength. Lieut Clute the only commissioned officer in my Co A present, and who had acted bravely, was seated near me. Turning round he remarked, "Boys they have put a hole through my coat." Just then "Attention" was called and the word "Forward" given. As Jim Clute rose, he gave a groan – and fell back dead – hit by a piece of shell.

He was noble, brave, generous and beloved by all. He was a young man – a native of NY – and a few years previous to the war – settled in our town (Houston). He left Texas as Orderly Sergt – and was soon elected 2nd Lt. The whole company mourned his loss. The boys took off his watch and valuables, to send them when able to his Mother & Sisters at Buffalo NY. Will McGowan[12] – a native of Texas, good, noble and brave – took command of the company – he being Orderly Sergt. After Jim Clute was killed we advanced but a few paces, when our Col – J B Robertson was wounded – and the gallant Upton took command. When Col R was wounded, the cry arose – "We are attacked in the rear" & behold a Yankee command, came advancing and firing as they advanced, from our rear. The boys gave a whoop, and with fixed bayonets – started at a run for them. When in 30 paces of them, each Yank began to wave something white and bawling out "I surrender, have mercy on me." The boys went to work taking prisoners and I hauled in a freshly imported Dutchman who seemed inclined to fight – but I convinced him of the impropriety of such a move. The prisoners proved to be the 4th New Jersey – entire – Col., all officers, ten companies – colors and brass band.[13] They surrendered to the "Bloody Fifth." The Col of the 4th New Jersey upon his sword being demanded by Lt Col Upton – replied "I desire to surrender to a field officer." Col Upton had on an old pair of pants, a dilapidated pair of cavalry boots, and an old cotton shirt, a slouch black hat – a huge sabre, with a pair of six shooters – looking less like an officer than any of his men. Col Upton in his blunt way, told him that he was a field officer and "to give up in a hurry" and says Upton "If you dam Yanks don't surrender when my boys call on you, officer or not, you will get shot."

Col John Marshall of the 4th (Texas) while leading his boys, was shot down. Lt Col Warrick succeeded him, and shared his fate. Capt Keys of Co "A" 4th then took command, and fell badly wounded. Col Raines of 1st fell badly wounded. The 4th Txs. had charged the worst position and suffered the most.

The Yanks were fleeing – and retreating in a hurry – and the battle of "Gaines Mill" was over but now in time of peace – I shudder to think what the victory had cost.[14] I was with some 15 other of the boys – and 25 Georgians – placed over the 4th New Jersey, and as dark closed in, we started for Richmond with our prisoners. Being very young and boyish, an Irishman took great delight in argueing the question with me "My boy" says he – "You are all brave fellows, but you are fighting against the stars and stripes, and my little man, you will all fail." Not desiring to discuss the question I relieved him of his canteen and shared my last chew of tobacco with one of the prisoners. Now that they were in our power I sympathized for them. One of the Georgians grasping me by the hand, in tears of gladness said "Thank God, Texas, the day is ours."

As we started off with our prisoners, night closed the bloody drama, and though in going back to the rear we had to travel for a mile and a half of the battlefield – yet we could distinguish nothing, except as now and then we stumbled against a corpse across the path. Yet from every direction – came sorrow and human suffering. Yanks and Confederates, mingling their death groans together, torches could be seen flying about – borne by some afflicted soldier – seeking in the faces of the slain – a dear brother or kindered. *Thank God,* I felt, I have no one here dearer than a friend – no brother or relative to worry me in the hour of battle.

We carried the prisoners some six miles in the direction of Richmond – when we were relieved by a detachment of Virginians. It being too late to find the Brigade – Will George[15] of my company (A) and myself spread our blankets down, after feasting off of captured provisions – and wearied with the work of the day – we soon sank into a refreshing slumber – not however before I had thanked my God for His protection, which had been given me in dangers of the battle field.

By 7 A.M. we were up and on our return for the Brigade. After proceeding a couple of miles, what a sight greeted our eyes. We came upon the fields – where the bloody work of the previous day had been carried on. On every side lay the victims of Death – three Confederates to one Yank[16] – which attests the power of their position and the desperation with which we fought. Caisons, rifles of every patent – muskets – belts – knapsacks – cartridge boxes – ammunition – haversacks – and all the necessaries of war, lay scattered about as the Yanks had thrown them when we drove them from their works and chased them. The Southern dead were many!! Some were in the act of aiming – some about to ram the cartridges home – some were biting the cartridges – and in all positions could they be seen in cold embrace of death. George and myself moving on a mile farther, came into an oak grove and there beheld our fellow Texans – some dead – some dying – and others in awful agony. It was our infirmary. Leaving this sad scene we moved on, and soon came across the "old Brigade" – Cheerful, defiant and yet much reduced. As an incident of this battle, I noticed one of the company – Jim Riley[17] – as we were pursueing the Yanks, take deliberate aim at a "Blue Belly" and fire – and hitting the cartridge box of the Yank, he blew him up. The loss of the "Texas Brigade" was very heavy – though I do not know the number. The Brigade carried into the battle at least 4,000 men, and lost at least one fourth – killed and wounded.[18]

After joining the Brigade we moved off to a large house – near by – Genl Whiting & Genl Hood made their Hd Qrts there. I was immediately detailed to report to Genl Whiting – which I did – and with some ten others, we guarded "Hd Qurts." Genl Whiting allowing apple brandy to get the better of him, remarked "There is nothing worth a *darn,* but Genl Whiting and the Texas Brigade." We remained in camp here until Tuesday morning. On Saturday (June 28th) our boys fought the Yanks at "Cold Harbor." On Sunday & Monday at "Savage Station" and were victorious. As we were not even near the scene of action I shall not speak. On Tuesday morning, McLelland made his final stand at *"Malvern Hill"* confronted by Magruder's division[19] – which as yet had not been engaged – and as we slightly figured in this engagement, I shall briefly speak of it. The battle began on Thursday June 26 – at Mechanicsville – was continued on the 27th, 28th, 29th, & 30th – and was now on the 1st of July about opening at Malvern Hill.

{ 43 }

We left our camp early Tuesday morning, near the "Gaines Mill" battlefield, and took the road leading to Malvern Hill – and on our way passed over the battle ground at Savage Station of June 29th & 30th – and dead Yanks were lying thick around. Now and then an arm or a leg could be seen sticking out of the dirt-where our boys had merely excavated a little dirt, had tossed from 5 to 10 – in a hole. What is war in this picture, you can see *one* of its traits. We marched on by – and from the report of canon and small arms, knew that we were approaching the scene of action at "*Malvern Hill.*"

"Malvern Hill" is situated about 14 or 15 miles from Richmond, and very near the James river. In front of it for the space of a mile, are hills scattered about, and half mile to the right is a swamp. The country being old, of course, but little woodland is seen, and the battlefield was principally on the old farm grounds.

We marched on, and by 11 A.M. arrived near the battleground. We were halted in a woods directly near which was a field, in which several of our batteries were stationed and playing upon the enemy. While resting here, I in company with the some of my comrades – started for a pond near by with the intention of filling our canteens – for the anticipated battle, leaving our rifles with the company, thinking that by expedition we would be able to return before they left. But on returning we found the Brigade gone – and our guns not left – and in the mean time the Yanks had opened their guns upon these woods. Desiring to be with the command and in our places, we started off. Dodging at every step – we soon came to this field, mentioned before – and at the distance of half mile – lying down in line of battle – in the tall green wheat, supporting our batteries we saw the "Texas Brigade," and we made our way to them over a bloody track. Where they had marched, could be seen, dead, and wounded men. One shell alone – in the 1st Texas, killed and wounded 27. No less than 4 different Yankee batteries were playing on the position which we were occupying. On arriving at the company, we were told that our guns had been left – and at a double quick we made our way back to the woods and by faithful search found our rifles. In passing through the woods, I noticed a singular circumstance – a Confederate soldier had taken shelter behind a big oak tree – two feet at least in diameter, and a canon ball, oblong shape – had bored itself through the tree, almost with

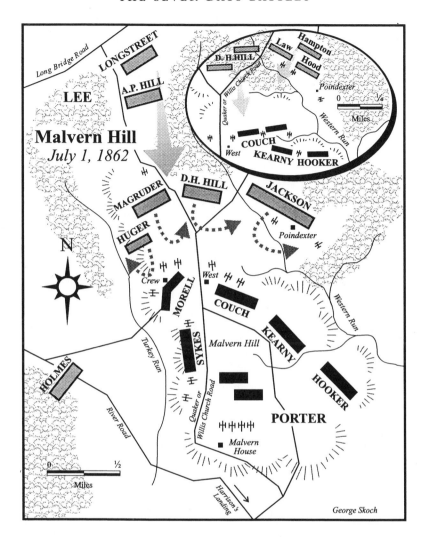

Malvern Hill
July 1, 1862

George Skoch

the precision of an auger, and had shattered the mans head in many pieces, scattering his brains on the ground around.

We soon found our way back to the Brigade, with an occasional bomb passing near and around us. About 2 P.M. – a detachment from each regt was sent out – all under the command of Lt. Col Upton – and ordered to move into the woods on the left and reconnoitre. Capt Turner[20] of Co "K" 5th Txs – took a detachment out on the right – and moved around on the flank of the enemy and engaged them. The battle was now fairly open – Magruder was charging bravely – and though his men were falling like hail, and his path strewn with dead and dying, yet he moved on – and victory was his. About 3 P.M. when Magruder began his bloody assaults, the batteries which we were supporting, opened upon the right flank of the enemy, and "Oh ye gods and little fishes," if we didn't ketch it – no soldiers ever did. No less than five land batteries, in all some 30 pieces, and three to six gun boats – by land and water at least 50 canon. What a racket it did make, just to think of it even makes me want to run. Our batteries replied – as long as they were able. Several of our guns were disabled and half of the horses killed – besides many of the artillery. Our Brigade hugged the ground laying perfectly flat, yet dispite this every few seconds you could hear the cry sung out "Litter corps here, Litter corps here" – and some poor fellow reeled over.

Directly we were compelled to draw off one of our batteries – and move ourselves more to the right. About 5 P.M., perhaps later, we got a position for one of our CS batteries – a good deal to the right, on a commanding eminence & it did such pretty firing and such good execution among the Yanks – that no less than 25 pieces concentrated on this alone but it stood the racket. McLelland had sustained another defeat today, and though he still held Malvern Hill, the positions which extended from the Hill to James river, had that day been carried by Magruder, and not only was the Yankee rear in danger, but the capture of their army a probability.

That night we still kept our position, and as soon as dark set in – all the Yankee gun boats, and Yankee batteries opened upon our position – with our guns replying occassionaly. The very Earth shook – and the whole heavens were filled with flying balls of fire – screaming and tearing through the air & bursting with hideous noise. We lay close to the ground – and went to sleep, with the missles of death flying around us. We had been under fire the whole day – and had lost some 50 men,[21] though we had not engaged their Infantry. By 1 P.M. the fireing had ceased, and we were withdrawn, in the "small wee hours" to a camp in the adjacent woods, where we were soon asleep again.

On being aroused early next morning, we found that the enemy in our front had left. During the day canonadeing and heavy musketry was heard in the direction of the James river, at a point between Malvern Hill and the river. It turned out to be a heavy battle between portions of the Yankee Army, and Magruders and Hugers[22]

Divisions of the Confederate. Magruder had on the day previous carried their works, connecting Malvern Hill and James river which movement necessitated their evacuation of Malvern Hill, in order to save their rear. Genl Lee knowing that they would in their present condition make for Harrisons Landing, some 5 miles below on James river, where their fleet and transports were anchored, had ordered Genl Magruder to extend his line parallel with the river, between the river and McLelland at Malvern Hill – and also ordered Genl Huger, (who had a large fresh division, as yet not having been engaged) to move to the right of Magruders division, which had it been done, would have cut McLelland off from the river and his fleet, his *only* salvation, and Lee and Jackson would have been in front and flank – and a few days would have seen the surrender of the "Army of the Potomac" Major (General) George B. McLelland commanding. Magruder took the position assigned – night July 1st but Huger, did not appear until after daylight – for by the time he arrived – all he could do was assist Magruder, who was fighting them. McLelland evacuated Malvern Hill, leaving many pieces of artillery, fought Magruder as a feint, in the interim swinging his forces around by the left, marching *un*disturbed to "Harrisons Landing" over the *very* ground which Huger should have occupied to cut McL off. By 3 P.M. – July 2nd McLelland and the remnant of his once proud and arrogant army, were safe under the guns of their "men of war" and river gun boats. I shall not speak of the "surprising Order" McLelland issued – seated safely on a gun boat deck – congratulateing his men – for their bravery – the heavy losses they had inflicted upon the enemy, and the famous manner in which they had "changed their base."[23] Allow me to say, that he could have changed his base – from the trenches of Richmond to Harrisons Landing – two months, one month, yes one week before he did, without the loss of a man or a gun.

But *now*, that "*base changing*" had cost him thousands of lives, of wounded, of prisoners, for no longer than the third day of the fight, I myself saw two and three Confederates guarding one and two hundred Yanks. I even saw squads of from 10 to 100 Yankees – alone, without a guard, making their way, to "Libby Prison" in Richmond.[24]

Stores – ammunition, arms of all kinds, canon – and every thing belonging to war, were captured from the Yanks. In charges that we made, we would sometimes chase the Yanks through perfect villages of tents – laid out with streets, and abounding in Yankee notions of every discription, as well as provisions of all kinds. On Wednesday evening we went into camp – and as we had been marching, fighting and maneuvering for seven successive days, independent of our trip from the Valley, you may rest assured that we were worn down, and for two days having had nothing to eat, we had "sorter keen" appetites. The 7 day battle we knew was ended, so we hoped our camp would be permanent, but no such luck – for on Thursday morning, in the hot broiling sun – we commenced the march for Harrisons Landing, where "Little Mac" lay, with his demoralized Yanks. We halted in some three miles of the Yanks – for it would have been dangerous to have advanced nearer in daytime – for a whole creation of gun boats would have opened on us. By dark we started for the Yanks. We arrived in a half mile of them, and relieved a Brigade of Alabamians who were on picket. All movements were conducted very quietly. My whole Co (A) from my regt (5th) was detached for picket and with the stealth of robbers. We proceeded a quarter of a mile, when we found the Alabama pickets lying flat, along a rail fence which enclosed a long but narrow field – some 125 yards across – the other side was bordered with a heavy woodland – and on the edge of it were the Yankee videttes, with telescopic rifles. We relieved these fellows. Co A – was stationed on the extreme right, and the details from the other regts – along on our left – giving to our Brigade pickets, at least a mile & half to guard. Omally (my mess mate) and myself, took a post together, for two men on one post was ordered. We took our post, to stand until 1 A.M. – and then two others of the Company were to relieve us. We lay down in a fence corner – (for the whole line had orders to lay down, keep hid, and make observations). We kept an eye through the fence – in the direction of Mr. Yank. By 9 oclock – the most awful noise I ever heard – began among the Yanks. About ten thousand axes began to chop – 3 or 400 brass bands to play – men began to sing songs, to cheer to laugh – and every other dam noise you can imagine – by mid night it ceased. By 11:30 I could hardly hold my eyes open, it seemed as if I had lost all control over myself. I would knod, my head would fall over, & Omally would . . . me and say "Bob – you asleep?" "Oh no," says I arousing myself. I looked through the crack to see ahead and in doing so – had to shut one eye. The other followed suit, and the first thing I knew – Omally was shaking me – crying "Oh you rascal – been asleep hey – I will have you shot." I raised up my head, and looking my messmate in the face, said "The hell you say. I have not been asleep, but have been watching through this crack at the Yanks." Omally was a good and generous soul and a warm friend of mine, he had let me sleep for nearly an hour, and woke me up, some 15 minutes before the relief came round. The penalty for sleeping on post is *Death*. . . . it what it may, the hardships of the past week – had worn me out and nature asserted her rights. We were all up next morning by daylight, in expectation of being relieved by some other company of the Regt. In order to find out if the Yanks still picketed across the field – Thos Fitzgerald and Dempsey Walker of "our mess" – both gallant young soldiers – were ordered forward (By their request) to reconnoitre the position. They moved forward very carefully and reached [the] opposite side of the field, and *met no enemy,* and moving on . . . out of sight. They were absent about an hour, and returning reported that the enemys nearest pickets were seven hundred yards off, having been withdrawn during the past night, from the position they occupied on the opposite side of the field. By 9 A.M. orders came for all the pickets to withdraw and join the Brigade, which we did by 10 A.M. Genl Lee had concluded to leave the "Young Napoleon"[25] to his glory, and to withdraw to the works near Richmond. We commenced the march, and in two days reached the suburbs of Richmond – where praises of "Hoods Brigade" were sung by all – making us feel proud of the part we had played in the 7 days fight. In our march from "Harrisons Landing" to Richmond we passed over the fields of battle – and from the first until we reached Richmond – our eyes grew dizzy by the sight of so many dead horses, mules and unburied Yankees, in a state of decomposition and very fetid.

Canon carriages – muskets, rifles, drums, tents – and wars necessaries were scattered both right and left. Genl Huger who failed to come to time, and cut off McLelland, *was relieved,* and never was through the whole war afterwards, *in the field. He should have been punished* more severely. On arriving near Richmond, we moved by the right flank and marched to a point on the Virginia Central RR, two miles from the City and pitched camp. It was the same place, occupied by us the night previous to battle of "*Seven Pines.*"

Chapter 6

"CAMP THUNDER

AND LIGHTNING"

$\mathcal{W}$e arrived at this camp on the evening of July 8th and from having experienced a rough time in it from a storm we called it "Camp Thunder and Lightning." On the morning of the 9th – tents were issued to the companies and the grounds divided off, and in a couple of hours our Camp had the appearance of a little village. "Our Mess" now besides Owen OMally – W P Morell – T W Fitzgerald, Dempsy Walker and myself, had a temporary addition of Mr. Watkins,[1] the aged patriot of the company – his beard and hair being almost white. He was an eccentric old chap, and of course we had "our fun." He was famous for stragling and foraging.

The first thing to which we devoted ourselves, was "skirmishing," which being translated means – "hunting War Bugs," alias "Army Lice," which on account of the past active days and weeks, had accumulated – to large numbers, all sizes and all colors. As for myself, I had but one suit of clothes to my name and I had been wearing them for *six weeks* dead ahead. Soon our camp was filled with goods, and in a few days each "reb" had on a clean shirt and a brand new suit of "Confederate uniform," and a new pair of shoes, for we had become almost barefooted. With clean clothes on, and plenty to eat, we began our important operations.

"Camp guard" was inaugurated – drills in morning and evening, roll calls three times a day, and a general inspection of dress, arms and accoutrements on Sunday morning. At one of these inspections, the 5th Texas took the premium as being the cleanest, and if some of our fair Ladies could have then seen the said Regt – they would have exclaimed "*What dirty fellows*," but we beat the others. In about two weeks there were no less than four gambling tents or resorts in the 5th Texas above and besides in every tent you could see a game of Poker going on, from 1 to 50 . . . in our mess . . . won the money and we spent it and you may rest assured we lived gay – vegetables, butter, milk, chickens, turkeys, eggs and all of which we bought with our funds – butter $1/pound, chickens $1.50 apiece & so on. Here my messmate, Morell, had recourse to a strategy. The boys would get on the sick list, so they would not have to attend roll calls and then "run the Blockade" and go into Richmond. Pickets were stationed all around the City, and one to enter would have to have a pass from Genl. Hood, and passing these pickets without a pass, was called "running the Blockade." Morell had been on the sick list & had run the blockade and the Dr. finding it out – had reported him for duty so if he now went, he would be absent from roll call and would be put "on roots," or confined for a week to the guard house so he gets a large lot of mustard, makes a very strong poultice and applies it to his back – and in about an hour, he lays down, commences to groan most piteously. The boys sent for Dr. Roberts[2] and Asst. Surg., & he came into the tent.

"Well Morell, what's the matter?"

"Oh – oh – Doc. My – my, back is b-r-e-a-k-i-n-g-"

The Dr. pulls off the blister and finds Morrell's back perfectly raw, he recommends something and orders Morell to be put on the sick list. As soon as he had left – up jumped Morell, brushing his hair, tying on a dilapidated necktie, borrowing a "V" – he starts out to run the Blockade, and was gone four days. Col Robertson tried to break up the gambling tents – but the boys would obey orders by moving them from *one* place and setting them up, in *another.* About this time Lt. Col. Brown Botts resigned, to the joy of the regt. – and the gallant Major Upton became Lt. Col. – and Capt. Whaley[3] of Co. "C" became Major. After the death of the brave Lt. Clute, our Comp (A) had an election for 3rd Lieut. Private F. M. Poland,[4] and Orderly Sergt. Will McGowan – both brave and deserving soldiers, ran for the office – and Will McGowan became the 3rd Lieut. – and was ever loved by his comrades, though he was but 22, and Poland was near 30.

Capt. Keys of Co. "A" 4th Texas – became Col. after Col. Marshall's death. Capt. Cortin[5] of Co. "C" – became Major. Our Brigade was now composed of the 1st, 4th & 5th Txs. – 18th Ga. – and "Hampton (SC) Legion" – and we were all camped together. Brig. Genl. Law still commanded us and his own Brigade "as a Sub Division." After we returned from "Harrisons Landing," we bid adieu to "Stonewall Jackson" and he moved up towards the Rappahanock with his corps.

About the latter part of July, muster rolls were made out, and the troops were paid off. Getting a pass one day and going to Richmond, I anticipated a pleasant time – going to the "Ballard House."[6] I got a good old Virginia breakfast – and sauntering down streets, admiring all the "pretty store doings," I was startled by the command "Sieze that Texan," and turning my eyes from the show cases to the street, I saw a Major – with a guard of some 40 men, with bayonets fixed, and having under guard some 20 odd "rebs" whom I supposed he had taken in tow, because they had no passes. The way he knew I was a Texan, was by my cap. In those early days of the war – nearly every soldier had his Co "number of regt. and state on his cap in fancy brass letters." As soon as he ordered me arrested, I turned to him and said "I have a permit approved from my Captain to Genl. Whiting." "Makes no difference now, sir" says he – so deeming "discretion the better part of valor," I consented to go – so with a bayonet on each side of me I was marched through Richmond streets to the edge of town and placed in a "guard house." Watching my chance, I soon made my escape, and meeting with Col. Upton in the city, I said to him "Col., how is it that when I come here on proper papers, I am arrested and placed under guard?" "Let's see your papers." I showed them to him, he read them and turning to me he remarked "If they attempt to arrest you again, tell them you belong to the Texas Brigade, and that it is not far from here, and *I* will bring them in and show them how to arrest Texans." I saw that the Col. was about 3 sheets in the wind. He moved on down the streets, and a guard ran up against him and demanded a pass. Upton tapped the handle of his sabre once or twice and remarked "I am Lieut. Col. Upton of the 5th Texas, dam you, and this is my pass" and with that he passed on.

Carl Horn[7] and Sam Weber,[8] two of our comp. who had deserted, were caught in Richmond. Weber made his escape from our camp guard. Horn was tried by court martial, but was released for want of full evidence. A few hundred yards back of our camp was the "Mechanicsville Turnpike," and from 4 P.M. until nearly dark, every evening, this road would be crowded with little market carts, loaded with vegetables & market produce for the Richmond Market. After we had been in camp here some 3 weeks, our boys would towards evening repair in squads of 5 & 6, to this road and commence operations. Here would come a cart, loaded with vegetables, two of the crowd would get in front – commence a conversation with the vendor as to what he asked for this and that . . . and about that time those others of the crowd would set behind the vehicle and bearing all their weight upon the rear part, would tilt it up, and in all directions the poor mans vegetables would scatter. Not only the Texans, but Georgians and other commands acted thus, and it was carried to such an extent that the "city council of Richmond," appealed to the War Dept. and guards were immediately posted along the highway. I myself was stationed on the road, and made it pay too, by exacting a tax from the verdant ones of the marketmen. For instance if a cart came along with eggs and butter, I would say "My friend, I am put here to protect you, hand over an egg, and a big slice of butter." Sometimes they would be too sharp for me and " . . . time" would I get anything.

Eating, sleeping, drilling, standing guard, and gambling were the pastimes of the day, but little whiskey was drank, and I saw not one drunken man in the camp during our whole stay at this place. The Brigade now numbered some 3,500 to four thousand men.

Chapter 7

ROAD TO MANASSAS

On the morning of "August 12th" orders were issued to "prepare three days rations, send all surplus baggage to our depots in Richmond, strike tents and be ready to march." Of this order we were rather glad, for we had become wearied of the inactive and monotonous life of the camp. We also knew that an active campaign was about to commence, for Major Genl. John Pope, or the Yankee Genl. who never saw anything but the backs of rebels,[1] had commenced his advance on Richmond, treading over the same ground and taking the same course as persued by Genl. McDowel[2] at the beginning of the war.

Genl. Stonewall Jackson was watching his movements, and ready to pounce upon him, which he did about the middle of Aug. near "Cedar Mountain," and in a bloody battle of that name, won for himself and troops a brilliant name,[3] but I digress.

By 3 P.M. Aug 12th – we took up the line of march – with full haversacks and bouyant hearts. Nearly all of the Confederate Army had ere this, left the vacinity of Richmond, and were scattered from Orange Court House, to Hanover Junction. We moved on and camped the first night some 12 miles from Richmond. Early next morning we were on the move. Passing by Hanover Junction, we took a road runing parallel with the "Virginia Central RR," and in two days we found ourselves at Frederick Hall, where we had camped when with Jackson on our trip with his corps, previous to the "Richmond battles."

We remained here some two days, and right merrily did we enjoy ourselves. The reputation our brigade had gained in the late battles, found us many admirers among the "fair sex" and as a result – plenty of nice eatables.

With grateful hearts we bid farewell to our "Fredericks Hall" friends and started on the march.

We took the public road for Gordonsville and in ten miles, branched off, leaving Gordonsville to our left, and Louisa Court House to our right & took the course for Orange Court House, situated on the Gordonsville and Culpeper Rail Road. At our camp mid way, I in company with some six others, were sent out into the country and stationed on a farm to protect the "old Farmers" corn – and as guard at his hospitable mansion, I spent a pleasant time for a day or so. Continuing on, we marched off to the right, leaving Orange CH to our left, our direction was now for the Rappahanock River. Our march so far had been hard and severe. The weather was almost intensely warm, so much so that men would fall by the road side, over heated. The roads were very dusty, and as a consequence, the water was not the purest.

On the morning of August 22nd we heard the Rappahanock River. We had already crossed the "Rapidan" and "North Fork" rivers both branches of the Rappahanock, and now before we would be upon the banks of the Rappahanock, we would first have to cross "Hazel Run" a small river & a branch also of the Rappahanock. When in some five miles of this river, we observed that most of the army wagons of "Whiting's Sub Div" had halted – and we felt sure that we were going to camp, and rations were going to be issued, for we had been without food for nearly two days. But alas, we passed them by and moved on our way, but not rejoicing. By 3 P.M. we . . . the ford of "Hazels run" and in 30 minutes the battle of

"Freemans Ford" began. In a mile of the ford we saw the wagons all parked, and ahead of us could be heard the report of the rifle – "a frolic ahead, get your tickets boys, or the managers won't let you dance," sang out some willy fellow – who "didn't care a dam."

The 1st Texas was in advance, and the head of its column soon came up to the Ford. Genl. Hood was ordered to advance, and carry the position. I will here briefly explain in "my way" the topography of "Freemans Ford." The ford some 400 yards long, and the river is about 150 yards wide at this point. The banks are very abrupt on both sides – and in 20 paces from either bank, the timber begins. A force stationed in these woods, along the bank, ought to defend this ford. Hazel River makes into the Rappahanock, some few miles below, and at *this* point, the rivers are not more than a mile and a half apart.

Genl. Hood ordered us across – and though the enemy were in the opposite woods, and artillery bombs bursting around. The current swift and waist deep, yet we advanced across, and soon gave a "terrific yell," and started up the banks. The Yanks gave us a volley and broke, we chased them through the woods for a quarter to a half mile, when we emerged upon a large cornfield – green and in bloom. This field was three quarters to a mile wide and gradually sloped to the rivers edge of the Rappahanock – on opposite bank were many large hills. All these were bristling with canon, and just so soon as we came from the woods, into the field, these "War dogs" began to thunder at us. Genl. Hood soon had us in line of battle and we charged the Yanks, who had reformed in our front, and in the field. We bulged into the corn – yelling like wildcats – and soon had the "Cerilean Bellies" running for dear life.

A large hill was situated in our front – half mile off (our line of battle was now perpendicular to the Rappahanock, our right flank being some 12 yards from it) and it began, in conjunction with the batteries across the river, to pour their wrath in the shape of canister; grape and shell, around our devoted heads. After penetrating into the cornfield some 200 yards – and being unable to see ten feet ahead – Genl. Hood ordered a halt. We had halted and reformed our ranks, and were awaiting "further orders" when the first thing I knew, I was almost wheeled around. I heard a crack, and then cries and groans. Being only stuned I soon came back to myself, and saw that one shot, more certain than the others, had made sad havoc. The shell burst in Co "C" – mortally wounding Major Whaley, and badly wounded others. The cries and groans were awful. For an hour we stood in this position – with balls flying all around. Genl. Hood seeing that we could accomplish no good in this position, ordered us to fall back into the woods from which we had driven the Yanks. This piece of woods was situated on high and lofty ground, and from it we could clearly see the Yanks across the Rappahanock as they maneuvered – and could see all over the field. As soon as we had formed "line of battle" in this woods, a Confederate battery of 5 guns, came galloping up – and took position, and soon it was puffing and belching away at the Yanks who occupied the far edge of the field. In a few moments we heard a yell, and looking to the left, we saw Longstreet with his Division – in line of battle, marching upon the Yanks – who still remained on "our" side of the river, and after a few moments "hard work," Mr. Yank concluded to retire from his inhospitable neighbors. The enemies batteries on opposite side continued to thunder away at us, but we clearly saw that this was only to cover the retreat of their forces – for we saw their columns of Infantry and trains of wagons moving off.[4] The battle was now over – as far as a victory was concerned – so "*we*" that is us Texans, concluded to attend to the wants of the inner man. We were informed that our supply wagons would not come up, and you can rest assured "how sad" the news was for we had received nothing for two days our only resource now lay in the cornfield, which was breaking down with fine big roasting ears. Permission was granted to the soldiers to get some corn from this field – and in ten minutes, our side of the field was filled with boys, breaking corn, and bringing it to camp – although the Yankee batteries were commanding this field by their fire. Soon the camp was flooded with green corn, which had been procured at the risk of life. Orders were issued that no fires could be built, nearer than half mile back in the woods – this was a "hard one," for now we would have to eat it raw.

It was the novel sight, to behold two or three thousand men, all at once, devouring green corn, and the rapid manner in which it was done would make a horse blush. I "put away" about ten ears and some of my comrades swore that they had finished on a dead stretch – no less than 40 ears – *I said no more.*

The night of the battle we left our position about 11 P.M. – and recrossed the river at "Freemans Ford," and in about an hour, were established in camp – when we found our wagons – and every fellow gave a "shout." Laying aside "our trucks" (as a soldier calls his gun, accoutrements, blanket, canteen, & etc) we soon had a big fire – all over camp. I started for cooking utensils and "Private Omally" of "our mess" started for the "fresh beef." We were cuting our beef up – anticipating a "splendid hash," our skillet was heating, one of "the mess" had gone to fill our canteens, another to draw our flour, and when to the surprise and disgust of all – the "*Long roll*" beat, and the cry went round – "prepare to move" – "carry cooking utensils to the wagons." "Eternally dam this Confederacy and hell fired Army" – was not whispered – but spoken by nearly *all,* in the passion of the moment. We had been marching for nearly three days without rations, had that day fought a battle, and were now not only deprived of something to eat, but of necessary rest. I pitched the dam beef into the fire – and then repenting sprang after it. Each soldier cutting him a slice – broiled it, and half raw, without salt – made a meal.

Soon we were ready, and the command "Fall In" was given and we were soon on our way. Hardly had we started, before heavy rain came on – and then began the tug of war – steping up – falling into mud holes and ditches – runing against some fellow and knocking him down – a nice time. About 3 P.M. we halted and lay down to rest. At daylight we were on the march again – and continued the march until 4 P.M. – when with weary limbs, we went into camp. We were nearly starved, we could hardly stand on our feet, so worn out and fatigued were we. We suffered for want of rest – both mental and physical for we had seen no sleep for nearly 40 hours. Why we were marched so hard without food, rest, or intermission I could never find out. The Yankee army I knew was before us, and falling back towards Manassas, and we were on his rear, but other troops were in advance of us and why the necessity of marching us to death. Genl Jackson was again in their rear. He had moved around in their rear, while they were disputing with us the passages of the Rappahannock and its fords. He had captured and destroyed immense stores – and was playing havoc generally with Major Genl. John Pope's rear communications. Our course so far, was in the direction of the Manassas Gap Rail Road.

We went into camp – a bountiful supply of provisions was issued – soon our fires were ablaze – skillets warm, and "good old
bread" and splendid fry, were the immediate consequences. After
having puffed away on our dear old comforter, "the Pipe," for an
hour, we took off our hat and shoes, and in company with the rest
of our comrades were soon in the realms of morpheus. Our rest
that night was sweet and undisturbed – nor were we aroused the
next morning before 8 A.M. This was Aug. 26th,[5] and after cooking
our breakfast and cleaning our guns, which had become rusty from
the late rains, we prepared ourselves for a . . . or anything else,
which might turn up. When to the surprise of all, orders were received to leave a detail of one man for each mess, and the remainder prepare to march. Before we left – 3 days rations were issued,
for the detail to cook up – Dr. Howard[6] – one of the company who
had lately joined "our mess," was left as *our* representative. As we
were on the line of moving off – Major Genl. J. E. B. Stewart, the
"Virginia Cavalier," rode up – and as he did so, for some reason we
halted. Directly I saw Genl. Jubal Early[7] ride up, and several other
officers – and were passing a large military blue coat around.
Curiousity drew myself and a few others to the seat of attraction,
and what should we find, but Genl. Stewart in a late raid had captured Major Genl. John Popes fine dress coat – and many things
belonging to that Yanks "dressing care," and by way of retalliation
was displaying them, for Genl. Pope had but a few weeks previous
captured Genl. Stewarts fancy cavalry hat – with its plumes & "doings" on it – as the soldier says – in 5 minutes the whole Brigade
was around old JEB – and Genl. Popes coat was thoroughly in-
spected. We moved on – taking a branch road, to the right from
the main Brentsville road – after proceeding some five miles – we
came to a halt. Details from each company in the Brigade were
made and marched off to an advance of half mile and placed on
post – as advance pickets on right flank, from fear of a cavalry force.

We picketed until daylight next morning, when we were ordered
to relieve our pickets and prepare to march – which we did in quick
order. After moving a couple of miles, we were halted and informed
that our rations would arrive soon. In about 30 minutes, here came
the detail, whom we had left the day before to cook up the rations.
Doc Howard, came up to the company – puffing, blowing and

perspiration pouring down his face – and a big sack on his back, which sack "we of our mess" knew to be *our* rations. Howard walked up to us – pitched the sack off in an excited manner – and exclaimed "Boys, I'll be damed if *I* will ever be on another detail to cook *all night* and now I have been walking for three hours with infernal load on my back, looking for this hell fired Brigade, so when you want the rations cooked again – *Howard* aint in." We all broke out into a big "horse laugh," for though we felt the truth of what he said, we were amused at his style and disgust, for he himself had proposed to the mess, that he should stay. As soon as all the companies had received their rations, and they had been distributed, we were ordered forward – taking direction a little North by West – in other words – aiming for Manassas. This was August 26.

We proceeded on – and as Pope with his minions was far ahead and no enemy near us – of course no incident very exciting, rather *bloody* took place, consequently I shall speak of the march of the next two days – in a very succinct manner. From 12 M – August 26th we continued on the march – seldom halting for the purpose of rest. When night had arrived – we were in hopes that a camp would be designated and we would be able to rest our wearied limbs, but as the soldier says "*No go.*" In other words we were destined to be on the tramp during the whole night. Until 10 P.M. the boys kept up pretty well – and some one, more happy than the rest, was continually cheering us with a ". . . song." By 12 M – the men began to drop off – worn out and unable to move farther – and at 2 A.M. for miles back, the roadside were lined with sleeping Confederates who unable to move farther had fallen by the road side.

By this time (2 A.M.) the *whole* Brigade would hardly make a decent company. My own Regt. had not more than 40 men on the move – and my Company (A) which was left centre company was almost upon the heels of Col Robertsons horse – and the flag was right upon him. I had kept up, despite the remarks of my comrades, "That sickly – slim built boy can't stand hard service." It is true, that when for a moment we would halt to rest, that I would fall off to sleep immediately as soon as sitting down, but when the orders "Attention – Forward" were given – I would start off – brought around by some comrade. At one time when we had halted – I felt myself going to sleep, as I was sitting down, and to me it seemed but a *moment* I was awaken by the marching of troops, and found that my Brigade was some 500 yards on the road. About an hour before day we were halted on the road side and ordered to sleep. By day light the "long roll" was beat – and we resumed the march – but you can rest assured that an oath was upon nearly every lip. During the hour that we had been asleep – a good many of our comrades who had fallen off in the first part of the night, rejoined us. After we had marched some three miles – a halt was ordered – the command "front" was given, and we made sure that we were going into camp – but how fallacious are hopes at times. Genl. Hood rode to the centre and his loud and martial voice made the following remarks – "Soldiers! We have a position assigned for us (Whitings Sub division) in the regular line of battle – our delay at "Freemans Ford" and picketing in the vicinity has thrown us out of *our* position, which is *one of honor and danger.* By marching on, and not halting to rest, we will by night regain that position. Soldiers, will you move on or shall we rest?"

"On – *On* – *On*" rose from every voice. The manner in which Genl. Hood spoke – and the hurried march of the previous night, all indicated that Genl. Hood and his boys of Texas had an honorable but dangerous post to take in the coming battle – which would be assigned to others did we fail to reach the position in time, at least this is an individual construction. We marched on, and by 4 P.M. we approached the "Blue Ridge Mountains" in the neighborhood of "Thoroughfare Gap." When in some mile & half of the Gap, we were informed that the Yanks intended to dispute its passage – and Genl. Fitz John Porter,[8] with artillery and infantry, now held it against us. The advance of the wing of the army to which we were attached had in conjunction with Lieut. Col. Upton (of our (5th Txs) Regt who had some 50 men under him from the Texas Regts as advanced scouts) had attacked the gap and driven him to the farther end (on Manassas side) and in this condition we found affairs when we arrived. After the Yanks had been driven to [the] farther end, and before our arrival – Col. Upton with his detail had ascended the Blue Ridge and was endeavoring to reach the other side, which he did safely. After arriving at the gap – we were halted and for half an hour we listened to the battle of "Wars Alacumes." Directly "Attention" was called and *we too* began the ascent of the

"Blue Ridge" a task by no means easy for men who had been on a forced march for 36 hours, without rest or sleep. We slowly worked our way up – pulling by bushes – stones and bending trees and by 1 P.M. (Aug 27th) the head of the column reached the turning point – when we were halted. The sound of the canon and musketry which proceeded from the gap – seemed as if it was coming from miles below us – when in truth it was but from 5 to 100 yards. Besides the firing could be heard the report of canon – and the glare from them could be seen – *it* proceeded from Genl. "Stonewall Jackson" who was in the neighborhood of "Manassas Junction" a point which he had reached by moving in *his* rapid way, around Pope. He had destroyed millions worth of war materials for the Yanks. His present position was a critical one, unless we could carry this gap – and reinforce him, for as he now stood – the whole Yankee Army was between him and Genl. Lee with the main Confederate Army. After halting on the top of the mountains a few moments, the order "about face" was given and we began to descend the side which we had just ascended. "Who in the hell commands here" "Does Genl. Hood know what to do" and such expressions testified the disgust of the men at these moves and counter moves of the Genl., seemingly to them, indecision on the part of the commanders. We at length reached the base – and moved by the left flank, into the gap – the 18th Georgia leading the advance and the "Hampton Legion" bringing up the rear. After we had moved into this rock walled excavation – a few hundred yards, we halted upon the Rail Road (for it runs through this gap – Manassas Gap Road). The fireing ahead at the other end of the gap continued. When we turned back from crossing the mountains, we were informed that the gap was cleared – *this indeed looked like* it. We remained halted nearly two hours – and the time was passed by listening to a long yarn – spun out by a favorite comrade of Co "*A*" – who possessed the not very euphonious nickname of "Blossom."

The fireing by 10 1/2 P.M. had entirely ceased and we were ordered forward. Not a sound was heard – every man held his breath as well as his voice – expecting every moment to be fired on by the Yanks in ambush. After geting wet to our waist – by wading a stream, we safely reached the opposite side – and came out up on Manassas plains. The Yanks had been forced to vacate this gap, by a force being sent around in their rear. No sign of the "Blue Bellies" was visable, except a few dead and wounded, lying on the road near the entrance to the gap. We marched on some 500 yards, perhaps it was a mile, and lay down to rest. That day on the march I was put in possession of a letter from home – giving me the notice of a brothers death. What a place I was in – with such sad news! The men lay down to sleep – and during the night nearly all of the stragglers came up and joined their respective regiments. In this march 3 out of every 5 had fallen off – from pure exhaustion – and unable to march farther. All were up now.

Chapter 8

SECOND MANASSAS

$\mathcal{B}$y 8 A.M. (Aug 28th) we were up – quite refreshed after eating our breakfast, consisting of two crackers and a slice of bacon. We prepared to march. We moved on – and in a mile, struck a line of timber – half mile through. As we were proceeding through this timber, a prisoner was brought us – and turned over by Genl. Hood to Templeman[1] – a noted scout of the Brigade – and a member of Co. "H" of the 5th Texas. Templeman carried his prisoner back to the gap (2 miles) and halting him, pulled out his six shooter, and sent his capture to Plutos dominions – or somewhere else. Nor is it out of place to give in a succinct form – the sad end of Templeman, rather an end – which from all circumstances considered – is worthy of study since it proves the verity of a biblical passage which quotes "Thou who lives by Blood shall by Blood die." This is the substance of the passage though not a "verbatim et literatim" transcription. Templeman was killed dead – 12 months afterwards – by the Yanks – near the *very spot* where he had in cold blood shot down his powerless and unarmed prisoner. After passing through this wood – rather passing to the other edge – we had a fine view of the old "Manassas" battle of 1861. On our right and left we found troops already stationed and a cavalry command were occupying the ground which we were to occupy. We relieved them and they moved to the rear. After joining our right and left with the forces on right and left – we found ourselves within 200 yards of the edge of the woods. A company from each regt. was ordered forward to occupy the front of each regt. as pickets – and to move to the edge of the woods and there station themselves. Co "A" from 5th Txs. was se-lected and under our Capt – D. C. Farmer – we moved forward and occupied the edge of the woods, each man selecting for him-self a good tree – as the Yankee skirmishers, some 800 yards distant began to fire upon us. As far as the eye could stretch – the Yankee line of battle could be seen. Pope had halted and on the bloody ground of 61 – intended to make a repetition of crushing the "Re-bellion."

The Battle of "MANASSAS NO. 2"—Aug. 29th/62

It is useless to suppose that a *private soldier* – in the ranks, could form an idea of the topography of the battle field, except in his own immediate ground – nor could he form a correct idea of the troops engaged – what position this Division or that division occupied – his duty, his work, lay right before him – and having nothing to do with right or left – he could not correctly make statements con-cerning a line – extending from right to left – some 8 or ten miles. Consequently I shall devote myself to the part played by "Hoods Brigade" and speak only of the ground over which they marched.

This wood in which we lay extended some four miles to our left – and was occupied all through by Confederates. In our front – at a distance of 800 yards, was a body of timber, running parallel for some three miles, with the timber which we occupied. Between the timbers was a large field extending from wood to wood – and on the Enemys side was enclosed by a fence. In the edge of these two separate bodies of timber were stationed the skirmishers of the Yankee and of the Confederate Armies. Half mile to our right, was a large hill – near which, and if I remember correctly, was situated the "Chine House,"[2] so famous in the history of this battle. Genl. JEB Stewart had occupied this hill, with a portion of his cavalry – and some few pieces of 12 pounders. This body of woods which the Enemy occupied was some 250 or 300 yards thick, and their first line of battle occupied the edge of it, most distant from us – this edge nearest us, being occupied by their (Yankee) skirmishers and sharpshooters.

With this brief, but I must confess not very intelligent description – I will proceed to fight again in fancy the most exciting and grandest battle of the Southern War. "In my minds eye" I can now (nearly four years since) see each tree – each bush, and stone, (much less more important features of the position), as I saw them then – but nature has not blessed me with descriptive powers – sufficiently powerful to paint to the conception of a stronger mind, the scenes and incidents – yet why do I dwell upon *this* topic? None but friends and kindreds who from consanguinity ties will pardon the defects of one – who spent his youthful years upon the arena of war, and not beneath the improving rod of a pedagogue. By preserving my carcass from common dangers – my mind might now be brilliant – but away with attainments & honors won at the cost of duty.

By "12M" (Aug 28th) we had our position. The rifles of the Brigade were loaded, caped, and the boys were ready at any moment to *charge* or receive a *charge*. At 10 A.M. the fireing, both of artillery and musketry became very heavy on the left – which proclaimed that the "work of carnage" was raging under the supervision of "old Stonewall Jackson." The firing came within a mile of our (Hood's Brig.) position – and from that point to a mile below us, it was quiet except light skirmishing. Our position was on right centre – "Stonewall" commanded the left wing, and Major Genl. Longstreet the right wing. The battle on the left under Jackson, continued until 5 P.M. with success to our arms. The Enemy charged and charged again – but were met by steady and brave men, who gave not an *inch*. By 5 P.M., the soldiers on the left – were wearied and worn – and the enemy still continued to charge them. At the hour (5 P.M.) it became apparent to the Confederate commander in chief, that the Yanks, by our inactivity on the right, had determined on a bold and reckless move. They intended to have a small force in the front of our right wing, and drawing off the main body of their troops from our right, (their left) reinforce their right, and throw them "en masse," upon our almost exhausted right under Stonewall Jackson. This determination was thwarted in its incipient stages, by a countermove of Genl. Lee's.

As I stated before – Co "A" – was some two hundred yards in front of the 5th Texas – as skirmishers and pickets of said regt. Each of us had a tree – firing upon the Yankee pickets in opposite woods, whenever one of them was bold enough to uncover his front, at the same time taking care to preserve our own front and precious carcasses. While going through this routine our ears were somewhat astonished about 6:30 P.M. (28th Aug.) with loud and tremendous cheers accompanying the sound of arms, from the left – ere we had time to render an opinion as to the cause of said cheers, we were called to attention, and in a few moments the clarion voice of "Hood" rang forth upon the breeze. "Fix bayonets" "F-o-r-w-a-r-d-" and with a yell we set out for the Yanks, yelling more like "incarnate fiends" than rational human beings. As the order "forward" was given, we closely joined our right and left, with the other companies from the Brigade, who were on the skirmish line. We as Skirmishers – preceeded the Brigade nearly two hundred yards, but they closely followed – with their shouts and yells. When within some 150 yards of the woods, where our friends of "Union persuasion" had their pickets, they fired a volley into us – and throwing down their guns, broke like quarter nags. After passing from the field into the *Yankee* woods, we (skirmishers) halted until the Brigade came up, and each company took its place in its respective regiment. We moved on through this Yankee woods (some 200 yards) and came forth upon the *plains*. There we saw that this charge was not confined to our "sub Division," but extended from extreme right to extreme left. The forward move of the right wing, had held to our front the Yanks designed to reinforce their (Yanks) right – and as we moved forward – Stonewall gave the order "*charge*" to his battle wearied soldiers – and the *whole* "Confederate Line," swept forward at one and the same time – as far as the eye could see. As we emerged upon the plains, could be seen the moving of "Rebs" and "anti Rebs" – the flash of hundreds of canon, and of thousands and tens of thousands of rifles. Add to this the report of battle, the moans and screams of dead and dying, the fierce yells and shouts of charging

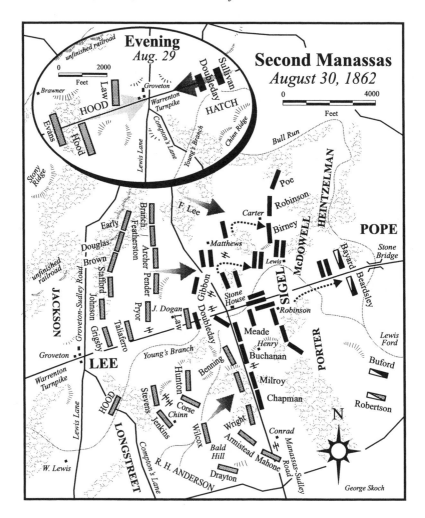

Evening
Aug. 29

0   2000
Feet

Brawner

Second Manassas
August 30, 1862

0   4000

Feet

George Skoch

"rebels," the tame "huza" "huza" "huza," of the Vandal Yankee –
and tell me what you think of war. Not long did we enjoy this
scene – by the rays of the sun – for it was nearly night when we
began the charge – and by the time we had routed the Yankee skirmishers – halted and rejoined the Brigade, and moved upon the
main line of the Yankee battle array. Night had drawn the sable
mantle on this earthly scene of international contention, but yet –
the battle went briskly on – and then, as the last ray of the depart-
ing sun disappeared beneath the western horizon – then began a
scene – which for grandeur – beauty and terrible beautiful – can be
described only by the pen of a Byron or a Pope – to render it easy to

the conception of one not acquainted with the "scenes and sights" of a battle field. For miles and miles around, in all directions a light more brilliant than that of day, shed its radiance upon each and every act of this bloody drama. Canons were belching forth their iron mission of death. The whole heavens were filled with thousands upon thousands of balls – and it was a beautiful indescribable sight to see the "bombs" and "grape shot" and shell – as they flew through the air with their unearthly noises – followed by their fiery tails – resembling fiery comets. We moved on – charging – yelling, and fireing driving the Enemy before us at every point. By 8 P.M. we had reached a small creek known as "Little Bull Run" – and this time "confusion was worse confounded." Brigades got mixed. Confederates began to fire upon Confederates. Yanks were passed over and fired upon us from the rear. On reaching "Little Bull Run" – a halt was ordered – and a regiment in our front fired upon us – and we were returning the fire, when the cry arose "We are fireing on our own boys." It turned out to be a Virginia Regt.[3] Then we exchanged shots with some command in our front – left oblique – the cry was raised "Hampton Legion" "Hampton Legion" "for Gods sake boys don't fire" and so it did prove to be the said "Legion" – who was the extreme left of our Brigade. A regiment moved by our left and were challenged by the 4th Texas. "What command?" "5th Texas" replied the cute Yanks – who had heard our name called – when we got into the fracas with the Legion a few moments before. Of course the 4th not suspecting anything allowed them to pass, and they joined their Army. The Enemy were now retreating. Our whole line, from right to left, had pushed them back. By 10 P.M. all was quiet – and the men seated themselves upon positions held, awaiting further orders. Near 11 P.M. – Capt. Harvy Sellers[4] – Aadj to Hood (and who came out from Houston as 1st Lieut. of my company) came up to our regt and gave Col Robertson the following orders "Col – The Enemy are in full retreat and are doubtless five miles from here by now. The whole line will fall back to the original position held before the charge, (some two and half miles in our present rear) but a detachment of our Brigade will be left on this spot (Little Bull Run) as "out posts" merely as a precautionary step, for the Yanks I dare say are miles away by now. So you Col. will leave one company from your regiment (5th) and a company will be left by the Hampton Legion. These will be sufficient to accomplish our purpose. They will give notice, *in case,* the Enemy should advance during the night."

To our disgust – Co "*A*" was selected from the *5th.* We had been on picket during the whole previous day, and now we must – far from our Army – watch during the night. The line fell back – and our company, under Capt. Farmer – formed a junction with the company from the "Hampton Legion," which was under a Lieut. consequently Capt. Farmer being senior officer – took command of the whole – some two hundred. Before reaching "Little Bull Run" is a very high elevation – extending several hundred yards – from this elevation, a fine view of the country beyond "Little Bull Run" is to be had – directly beyond Bull Run for 100 yards the land is rather low, from that point it begins to enter upon a gradual ascension. Capt. Farmer with his own and the "Legion" company, occupied, this elevated place near "Little Bull Run" and stationed his pickets. I came on at 12M and stood until 1 P.M. when I was relieved by John McMurty[5] of the company. My time would arrive at 4 A.M. – to again go on post. After being relieved I took a "good ole smoke," and devoted a few moments to thinking of the past bloody hours – but I was soon asleep.

By 4 A.M. I was aroused, and again resumed the "lonely tramp of the sentinal." Some 12 others were on post – at positions equidistant at about 100 yards. Daylight broke on Aug. 29th as well as I can remember about 5 A.M., perhaps a little before. As soon as day broke, in fact as soon as an object could be distinguished ten paces from you – the whole company, with the South Carolinians of the Legion, were up and hard at work and what do you suppose doing? They were picking the pockets of the dead, dying and wounded Yanks who lay thick and numerous around us – and numerous were the *silver watches, greenbacks, pocket knives,* and divers other *notions* with which our boys loaded themselves – taking care of the "inner man" by borrowing from our helpless friends all the "hardtack," bacon & etc. – with which they were possessed. When day had so far broke that we could see several hundred yards beyond "Little Bull Run," we on the picket line, discovered in this "flat" beyond "Little Bull Run" – a large body of troops – seemingly from the space which they covered, to be near 20,000 – but it was not sufficiently light to decide upon their politics. We were inclined to believe that they were "Confederates" since Capt Sellers had told us the previous night that no Yanks were in 5 miles of us and were in full retreat. To be prepared for any emergency – we examined the priming of our guns and made sure for ourselves. A few minutes would prove them friend or foe.

In about 5 minutes they discovered us, but were as equally in the dark – as to our "persuasion" – so they sent a horseman in full tilt towards us. He came within a few hundred yards of us and cried out "What People are you." Dempsy Walker of our company advanced towards him & in "Scottish style" – answered his question by asking another – though in less polite style "Who in the hell are you" asked Dempsy. With that our gallant horseman wheeled his stud, and in full gallop started for his command. As he turned about our impulsive but gallant Walker gave him the contents of his rifle – but on account of the distance – missed his mark, though he was a fine marksman. As soon as our horseman had reached his command – a great stir began in the *Yankee* camp – for such we *now* saw them to be – for it was becoming very light. Four or five pieces of Artillery were placed in position, and opened on us – skirmishers were thrown out and began to advance. A body of cavalry dashed off and began to circle around to cut us off. "Israel to your tents" Farmer immediately ordered his company under arms and the "Legion" company likewise. We who were on the picket line were called into the company, and Capt. Farmer formed a strong skirmish line – occupying a distance of several hundred yards – a space of 10 feet intervening between each man. The grape shot began to rattle around our head – the Yankee skirmishers were advancing – and in a few moments the Yankee cavalry (some 45 strong) came dashing upon our right flank – intending if possible to cut us off from our army and capture us. But we had no idea of "visiting the North," so in military style we gave them a salute – which sent them prancing back.

Some 200 yards back in our rear was an old and deserted field and to this Capt. Farmer ordered us to fall back to, remarking "Boys, we *must* hold this position at all hazards." We fell back – and along came the Yankee skirmishers – 5 to one of us, and backed by heavy lines of battle. The scene was by this time, quite lively. We were exchanging shots and their canon were making merry misses around our ears.

We took as good a defensive position after reaching the field as was presented, determined if possible to check the Yanks in their advance. On they came with their "Union cheers" confident of "gobbling" us up. We allowed them to come within 75 yards – when Capt. Farmer seeing that he would get all his men captured – ordered us to fall back several hundred yards, to a lane – which was bordered along with trees. The enemy line overlaped us – right and left – for half mile – besides their artillery was continually busy. As we were moving back quite leasurely – I was hit in the back with a spent grape shot – for my back as I walked off, was directly to the Yanks. It hurt me about as much as if it had been thrown by a child. We reached the lane, each man took a tree, and we again faced our foe. In this lane we saw a beautiful brass 12 pounder, which we had captured in our charge the previous night, but our boys when they fell back did not carry it off. We knew that the Yanks would now recapture it, for we were unable to carry it back with us. The Yanks advanced on us and we poured it – that is the "minnies" into them – but it was no use – they were flanking us on each side – so our gallant Captain Farmer ordered us to again fall back. This we continued to do – falling back and holding them at bay, until we reached our Confederate line of battle – which we found in the *same* position as on the day before. Our Brigade was lying in the same woods, with its skirmishers occupying the edge. As I mentioned in the beginning of this Chapter – a field intervened between the woods we occupied and that occupied by the Yanks. Within this field – within 500 yards of the Yankee picket line – was a deep ravine – much washed by the rains. As we approached this ravine an order came out to us, from Genl. Hood, to occupy it, and act as sharpshooters – which we did. I neglected to say, that when the Yanks reached the "beautiful piece of artillery" in the lane, they gave three tremendous cheers. On stationing us – Capt. Farmer went back to the Brigade and made his report to Genl. Hood. Thus two small companies had lain nearly a whole night within 500 yds of 20,000 Yanks – and two miles from *any* portion of our Army.

On the morning of the 29th, Pope was so elated that he was not destroyed – and to his surprise finding that we had fallen back, telegraphed to "Abe Lincoln," that the "Rebels" were fleeing before him.[6] This created such a splendid and happy feeling in Washington City, that a large party – nearly a hundred of the "Capitols" *elite* fashionable young gents – laid in a supply of liquors – segars – and delicacies – and started for the battlefield, to have a "gay time" concerning *these,* I will hereafter speak. Genl. Hood on this day, was put in command of two Brigades, besides his own.[7]

After occupying our position in this ditch, we began a slow, desultory fire with Yankee pickets, who occupied the edge of the woods opposite us – the same as previous day. Jule Robinson[8] – of our company – a brave young Delawareian, and Dempsy Walker, crawled upon their all fours to within 200 yards of the Yankee pickets – and laying down behind little corn hills – began to interfere with "our friends" across the way, to a considerable extent. They could not hold their "corn hills" long, for a few Yanks, more daring than the rest, had climbed trees, and in return, interfered with Messers Robinson and Walker to such an extent, that they were forced to return to the company. Myself and one or two others, climbed some trees – but found that we could do but little at it.

About 2 P.M. Gregory[9] – the acting commisary of the regt. came into the company with a supply of crackers and bacon, and on dividing them out – 3 crackers and 1/4 lb. meat fell to each man. I was very hungry – but I concluded that I would "husband my resources" and have a *big* meal that night at supper – but the sequel proved the error of this action – as we will see in time.

It was now about 3 P.M. (Aug. 29th) and the fireing on our left under Jackson was becoming very heavy. At 4 P.M. Genl. Hood rode up in a gallop in front of the Brigade – and Maj. Sellers, his Aadj galloped down the "Texas picket" line. In a few moments the cry was borne upon the breeze by the martial voice of old Hood *"Attention Texas Brigade"* "forward" "March" – and the yell was raised and off we dashed. Co "A" joined the skirmishers as they came up.

On we moved – treading over the same ground taken the previous day. Men were never more frenzied in their passions as our boys were. We reached the woods in which the Yankee pickets were stationed, and as we came near upon them they gave us a volley – and then dashing down their guns and all encumberances, made for their rear at first class speed. We followed closely upon their heels; and after passing through the woods for a few hundred yards, we were halted by the magnificent and fierce array of a Yankee line of battle – composed of the New York Zouaves[10] – from New York. The battle was now rageing from right to left. We *halted* but it was but for a moment. Our skirmishers were ordered to their regiments. Hood – Upton and our gallant leaders were at their posts. The Zouaves were at a charge bayonet – and when we were in 20 paces of them they fired upon us. The Yankee batteries too, were freely complimenting us. As they fired, our gallant, brave, generous and noble Upton – fell mortally wounded – from a Yankee shell. Sleep thou brave. No high flown compliment from this pen of mine can add to your fame, for it lives in the love and admiration of those who so oft had followed you upon the plain of carnage – and so long as one of the "Old Fifth" shall live – Upton will not be forgotten. As soon as the Zouaves fired upon us, Genl. Hood gave the order – "Fix bayonets" – and the rattle of steel rang down the lines. "Fire" "Charge" came in quick succession – the smoke of our guns had hardly rose from the pieces, when at the command "charge," we made for the Zouaves. As we rushed upon the Zouaves – with their blue jackets, red legged pants and yellow caps – they gave way, unable to stand the sharp pointed instruments with which we greeted them. Now came a scene of which my feeble pen cannot portray – a scene though mid the dangers and carnage of the battlefield – was yet beautiful to the observer. The ground on which the Zouaves stood, as I said before, was at the edge of the woods – from which woods began the great and beautiful plains of "Manassas." The ground from where the Zouaves were drawn up in line of battle began to slope gradually – for the distance of 300 yds. at which distance a clear and pebbly bottomed branch ran at the base of the slope. Passed this stream, the ground began to rise, breaking itself up into hills and valleys. As soon as the panic struck the Zouaves they threw down their guns – and in groups of 5 & 6 – to 10 – broke for this branch – and I speak candidly when I say, that before they had reached this branch – we had brought to the ground, half their number – and in crossing this branch – so much confusion attended their crossing that we made the branch run blood – and after crossing the branch we continued to bring them to the ground until from their own confusion. So 50 out of 1,000 got away unhurt.[11] Nor is this wonderful – for as soon as we had got them started – we followed right upon their heels – and would shoot into a crowd at the distance of ten paces. I remember one incident of this scene – as I was running along and loading my rifle – a Lieutenant of the "Hampton Legion," slaped me upon the shoulder in a very excited manner exclaiming "Yonder Texas – goes a beautiful crowd – shoot – bring one the dam devils down – shoot quick" – and as I fired, he gave a yell – hardly had the sound of his voice died out before he fell – "shot in the leg." "Give me a string, a rag – a hankerchief quick, for Gods sake quick." One of the boys handed him the desired article, and hastily seizing it, he hurriedly bound it around his leg above the wound – and jumped up – waveing his sword – he moved forward at a limp – yelling at every step.

It must not be thought that our victory over the Zouaves was bloodless to us – for several batteries of artillery were plying their missions into us – besides the fire of a heavy line of Yankee Infantry beyond the branch. Many a brave and noble Texan fell – our work was but begun.

After defeating and almost exterminating the Zouaves, we moved at a "double quick" and "charge bayonet," across the branch, and charged a second line of battle of New England Infantry.[12] They poured into us while we were ascending the bank, but when we approached them, with the cold steel, they gave way and fled – and *then* we slaughtered them. After ascending the bank upon which they were stationed – it being a considerable elevation – a view of the whole battlefield presented itself – and as far as the eye could see – front – right and left – the mingling of the "Confederate Cross" and "Stars and Stripes" – mid the yell of charging legions – the noise of arms, the screams and groans of the dying, greeted our sight. As soon as we had obtained this position – 3 Yankee batteries – supported by heavy lines of Infantry opened upon us – right, center and left. "On my boys" was borne upon the breeze – and at the word we gave a yell and charged. The 5th and Hampton Legion moving to the right, on the Artillery and Yanks in that direction. The rest of the Brigade (1st, 4th Txs & 18th Georgia) moved off upon the left – and from that moment during the rest of the battle, the seperation continued. On we moved – each step was marked by the fall of comrades – dead – dying and wounded – yet we paid no attention to them. A comrade as I passed him – fallen and bleeding – cried "for Gods sake aid me." My duty to the living and my country drove back the generous impulse of nature to aid him – and passed him by. When we were within some 40 paces of the Yankee canon – our "Lone Star" flag was seen to fall. Hardly had it touched the ground when the gallant sergt. Simpson[13] of Co. "A" grasped it from the hand of the dying Royston[14] – and waving it on high-moved forward, but only to fall himself a few paces farther on – severely wounded – and as he fell – he raised the "single star" on high – and young Harris[15] of Co. D bore it on – in a few moments to receive his death wound with that unfortunate flag in hand. On we moved, and in a few moments the Yankee support and artillery was flying from us – with the Lone Star and Palmetto[16] flags waving over their batteries. Halting but a moment, we rushed forward – for legions of Yanks confronted us – as we charged – line of battle after line of battle – victorious in each charge. Often could we hear the battle cry of the South Carolinians – "*Legion rally to your colors,*" and to a man they responded. After charging and fighting from some two hours – our men becoming too much disorganized we halted in a grove of woods from which we had just driven the Yanks and were reforming – when to our surprise the Hampton Legion – hardly taking time to reform, rushed forward with a yell – crying out as they passed – "Texans follow us" – and our men – excited by this – rushed forward with a yell – and by the Gods – we not only followed – but we *led* them as again we rushed upon the Yankee mercenaries. All along our lines the Yanks were pushed and we moved forward driving – killing and destroying the "Cerulians."

After moving out of this grove of timber, and attacking and routing several lines of battle – we descended to a valley in which was situated a "farm house" – defended right and left by a heavy line of battle – supported by some six pieces of canon. On we moved – yelling like fiends – and worked to battle rage – for half of our gallant regiment (5th) were weltering in their blood – in the long and successful career we had run that day. On we moved – and down our "Lone Star" flag would fall – but ere it reached the ground – seized from the dying by the living hand. We moved upon the farm house – and handsomely and bravely supported by the Legion – Georgians & Virginians[17] – we soon carried the Artillery and had the "blue bellies" on the run. As we entered the yard of the house –

about a dozen of us moved to the corner of the house on the left and opened fire upon the retreating Yanks thinking that our regiment was scattered through the yard. In about 5 minutes, hearing the cry "Forward" given – we turned about to join our regiment – but lo and behold it was many hundred yards off to the right – moving upon a fresh line of battle – and knowing that it was not a time for fastidious taste as regards *State,* I joined in with a regiment which was moving upon the Yanks – to the left of the house. On we went and when within some 40 steps of the Yanks, they fired a heavy volley into us, and this regiment which was a *Virginian,* turned and fled like dogs – and I followed suit – for there "discretion was the better part of valor." The officers cursed and swore, and endeavored to rally the regt. – but they could not stop them. When they had run some 200 yards, we came upon the 20th Georgia under the gallant Col. Benning,[18] and some few with myself deserted the Virginians and joined the sons of Georgia.

On we moved – upon the same Yanks from whom the Virginians had just fled – and though grape – canister, and minie balls were poured into us with destructive effect. Yet on we moved – and soon had the Yanks a fleeing – who seeing they could not carry off their canon, shot their horses. After carrying their position—we advanced into a woods near by and Benning halted us to reform. From this woods a plain sloped down for some 500 yards & then began to assend – extending to a farm house – some 400 yards from the center of the valley – and 900 from the woods we occupied. This farm house was on an elevation – and had stationed in the yard a battery of six canon – a battery on the right swept the valley. Within some 150 paces of the house was a rail fence which was lined with Yankee infantry. Col. Benning reformed us and looked at this position. "Boys, we must get them dam fellows away from yonder" and the plain but brave old Georgian meant just what he said. It was evident that the Yanks were whiped and that they were now making their last effort to prevent a total rout. "All right Colonel" said the Georgians, and I united myself with Co. "D."

The task was desperate – for we would have to charge nearly a *thousand* yards – with batteries playing on front and right flank, not considering the Yankee Infantry who were 5 to one – but old Benning with his 400 men determined to *try* them *any how.* "Forward Boys," said the Colonel – and as we rushed forward with our battle cry – he rode his old charger forward and led us. The batteries and Yankee Infantry opened upon us – and by the time we had reached the center of the valley, (500 yds) we had lost nearly one hundred out of 400 men – and the worst was yet to come. "Lay down boys – dam hard job" – said the Col. – and we all lay down. Impatient to see our situation, I got up from the ground – and was standing up, when a ball hit my right leg above ankle, and shattered my bone – and down I fell. "Fall back" cried the old Col. – who saw that he could not save a man, did he remain stationary or advance. Not desireing to be captured – I made an effort to rise – intending if possible to limp off on my well leg – and had made some 3 or 4 hops – when a true aim – again passed through my already wounded leg – some two inches below first wound – and I fell, unable to move.

The Georgians fell back to the woods. My God what were my feelings – home – loved ones – Yankee prisons and a lingering death flashed upon my mind. Near where I fell was a pile of rails – some 3 feet high – to them I rolled, after cutting off my blanket – cartridge box and accoutrements – and as I lay there – balls were hitting these rails about my head – hiting in the ground in a few inches of me, throwing dirt upon me. After laying there some 15 minutes – I was indeed surprised at the Yanks not pursueing us – but the mystery was soon explained – soon a shout rose upon the air – and too well I knew it – for it was the cry of our Confederates. They moved upon the flank of these Yanks at the farm house – and Benning moving by his flank – soon joined them and the temporary success of the "Popers" was dearly paid for – they ran – and soon victory was ours. The battle was now ended – for when I fell – it was near dark. The Yanks with their gallant commander – John Pope – were on a double quick for Leesburg and the Potomac – leaving canon – guns – tents – and everything valuable belonging to war. Demoralized and whiped – they fled – followed by the keen and telling sword of Genl. J. E. B. Stewart with the Cavalry of the Virginia Army. God had given us victory *His* name be praised.

Chapter 9

RECOVERY

*L*aying where I fell, as dark closed upon me, my feelings were anything else than pleasant. The last sup of water – so pleasant and necessary to the wounded soldier, had been drained from my canteen – and not only was my thirst great and unsatisfied – but the cry from dying & wounded that lay on every side – sent forth their sad cries "water, water, for Gods sake relieve my thirst." Soon after nightfall – I was joined by a wounded Georgian who made a Yankee – who was slightly wounded in the head, pack him on his back – and the Georgian – Yank & myself – formed one group – on that bloody field.

After dark had fairly set in – torches could be seen fliting to fro – held by the hands of the unhurt – searching for friends and relatives. A torch soon approached us & my wounded Georgian cried out "Hello John – this way." John marched up "Why Tom old friend – did they get you?" "Who are these you have here?"

"One is a Texan – the other a wounded Yank, whom I am making useful" replied Tom. "Oh yes, said John – I heard Lieut. – – –

of Co D speak of the young Texan" John soon left us for the camp of the 20th promising soon to return with comrades and litters and bear us off. By 10 P.M. John returned with several comrades & litters and they prepared to bear us to the field infirmary of the 20th Georgia. The pain I suffered in being lifted from the ground into the litter, can only be felt – but not described. On arriving at the field Infirmary – we were soon prepared for – in the shape of a straw pallet and a big fire – can I ever express the gratitude I feel and felt – to those good and brave men of the 20th Georgia. I was a stranger among them. My only claim upon their kindness being that I in a common cause had followed their flag – fought and fell beneath its stary folds. To me they were very kind. The assistant surgeon of the regt. – gave me his overcoat as a coverlid – for I had no blanket. The Lieut. of the company (D) in which I had fought – came to see me – and complimented me for the part I had borne. I remained there that night – and from 11 P.M. – a heavy rain fell upon us. The next morning my wound was examined – and the Doctor reported my leg badly shattered – but *perhaps* could be saved.

The next morning – a tent was raised over us – and about 11 A.M. – while in a dreamy state – which morphine always brings – I was disturbed by the entrance of a well known face. "Jim my old fellow how are you?" cried I as I recognized the features of the good natured Jim Downey,[1] litter bearer of my company – "Why Bob – my boy, I am sorry to see you thus – I have been looking for you all morning – the boys were getting uneasy." "Old Jim" as we called him, soon had an ambulance – and biding adieu to my kind Georgia friends – I started for the Infirmary of my own State.

After going a few miles – we halted and took in "F. C. Hume"[2] of Co "D" 5th a brave and gallant soldier. Soon we arrived at the Texas Infirmary – what a sight greeted my eyes – as I was borne from the ambulance – to a tent – around which lay many dead. Piles of arms & legs could be seen – and the death groans of comrades were heard. Oh Texas – dearly did you pay for the fame your sons won upon the plains of Manassas. Over 400 out of 680 – of my regt. (5th) had fallen – but we suffered more than any other regt. in the Brigade – except the Hampton Legion who fought side and side with the 5th after the Brigade got seperated.[3]

I was carried into [the] fly tent of my Company (A) and tenderly cared for by those of my comrades who were detailed as nurses. Some 20 lay around – some of whom were already in a dying condition. Some three or four others were outside – laid among the dead. What a scene! and what must have been my feelings to see around me in the cold embrace of death – those of my company who a few days before were alive and happy – with whom I daily associated – and who were to me brothers. The first evening of my arrival at our infirmary – I was startled by loud huzas and derisive laughter. Casting my eyes towards the road which ran near by – I myself – in pain though I was – could not restrain my laughter. Passing by under guard were 200 of Washington City gents who as I mentioned before – had left Washington with fine wines – segars and delicacies for a spree on the battle field when Pope's dispatch (after the first days fight) was received – announcing a *Union Victory*. They were marched to Richmond in their fine clothes – but our soldiers – they tell me, would not let them take their wines and "palate soothers." Such is life!!!

Our army pursued the Yanks – and invaded Maryland.[4] With them, for the present I am done – since the object of this work confines me to individual experience – whether on battlefields – in camp – in Hospitals or on a furlough. So whoever *may* chance to read this work, will pardon me for an adaption to the moves and motions of *self*. On the 3rd day – Dr. Breckinridge,[5] Surgeon of the 5th (and a cousin to Vice Pres. J. C. Breckinridge[6] – and also a native of Kentucky) collected his ambulances and prepared, in conjunction with the other surgeons of the Brigade – to move the Texas wounded to Warrenton – Farquier Co – distant some 14 miles.

Sam Bailey[7] and myself of "Co A" were placed in the same ambulance and started off for Warrenton. By 3 P.M. we arrived at this beautiful Virginia town and found most of the Texas wounded already arrived. Our road from the battle ground was over a rocky turnpike – and greatly did we suffer – jolting and rumbling – and both of us badly wounded. On arriving at Warrenton – as soon as our ambulance had stoped near a Hospital – several ladies (God bless them) began to cluster around – with all the delicacies of the season – and feasted us sumptuously.

Of those detailed of Co "A" to look after Co "A" wounded, were J. S. Norton[8] – James Lands[9] – James Nitherby[10] and Stephen Watkins, an old veteran, who was detailed for my especial benefit through the kindness of our Surgeon Dr. Breckinridge. J. S. Norton – the senior of them all – near 40 years old – was a thriving merchant in Houston & one of the most pushing, energetic and perservering men I ever saw – kind and gentle as a woman – and a general favorite with all the company. As soon as he found out that we were going to be moved to Warrenton, he started out in advance – and on reaching Warrenton went to work and obtained for Co "A"'s wounded, a large two story airy building. He got some cots – some matrasses – pillows, sheets – and coverings – made arrangements for milk daily – butter – fresh beef – mutton & pork – and dispatched Mr. Stephen Watkins, who was an adept at forging, on a foraging expedition. Mr. Watkins returned with a wagon loaded down with turkeys – chickens – butter – fruits – bacon – honey – preserves – and every delicasy – so when Co "A's" wounded arrived – Norton had a nice clean bed – and had our room fixed up in tip top order. To him we shall ever feel grateful.

An Ast. Surg. – Dr. N. J. Crow[11] – a kind and genial man, was assigned to us. Our company wounded amounted to some fifteen – some five to eight having died – together with those who were too slightly wounded to be treated. Rice – tea – coffee – flour-meal – sugar – wines – brandies and cordials were issued us by the Confederate Govt. The Agt. from the State of Texas arrived about this time – and placed a fund of several hundred dollars in the hands of Norton for our Company.[12] Capt. Farmer – forwarded several hundred more – from the "Company fund" – which money Norton devoted to our comfort in buying such things as the Govt. did not and could not furnish – in paying for our washing – and hireing servants. Every day – a bevy of fair Virginia Ladies were in our room – doing all that woman could to alleviate our sufferings. In fifteen days – some half dozen of our brave boys were corpses. The gallant Dempsy Walker, who has before been mentioned in these pages – ceased to live. James Witherly[13] one of our nurses – was taken from us – by the hand of death. The gallant Heflin[14] – De Young[15] – Angell[16] – and Massenburg[17] – had fought their last fight, and nobly had they performed their duty – at all times.

My wound was not doing well. I took chills and fevers – gangreene set in. The blood would when ever my leg was much lower than my body – spurt out – and run in streams – and I was forced to have my leg for a week at a time, suspended in the air – tied by ropes falling from the ceiling. The sufferings I underwent can not be described. Well do I remember a kind Motherly old Lady – with affection beaming from her countenance. Attended by her beautiful daughter – who would pay their visits to our room – seat themselves besides my couch – and smooth back my hair – and cool my fevered brow – talking all the time of my Far off Texas home – others would come in – and make me the recipient of their many and nicely prepared delicacies.

For four weeks I was confined to my bed – compelled to lay the most of my time on my back. Our life here was indeed pleasant, considering our condition and all circumstances. Ladies in great numbers visited us – and laying aside all reserve and ceremony, acted towards us as relatives, doing all to alleviate our sufferings. When one died – (and many brave men were daily passing away) they followed him to his soldiers grave. Surgeons were kind and attentive – and our nurses were as tender as women & as careful of our wants.[18]

About the 27th of Sept. – a pair of crutches was furnished me – and for the first time I rose from my bed – with an intention of trying to move about – but found myself so weak that my well leg would not support me – and for a day or two, I contented myself by crawling a little at a time around the floor – on one knee and my hands.

On the evening of 28th (Sept) Warrenton – soldiers & citizens, was excited to a high pitch by the hasty entrance into the town of a Company of Virginia Cavalry – who reported a Brigade of Yankee Cavalry advancing upon the town. There was a battallion of Infantry under Lieut. Col. Payne[19] – hospital nurses – wounded soldiers (several thousand) and the women, pardon me, Ladies, of the town. This comprised the posse . . . civic and military. The Yanks however did not come on the 28th, as our terrified Confederate Cavalry represented – and we began to think that it was but a figment – eminating from the fears of our Southern Cavaliers. Col Payne (the post commander) ordered all arms to be brought to the grand house

– as if *he* would make a fight. We did not remain long in suspense – for on the morning of Sept. 29th about 10 A.M. – a most awful confusion was raised. "Yankee Cavalry – Yankee Cavalry – here they come – Look out" – and as our room was immediately on the main street which passed through W. we of Co. "*A*" had a fine view. Hardly a minute had passed after the above cry was raised – before here comes about 40 *rebs* – who had been out on picket. Here they come – fleeing for dear life – whiping and beating their steed, with carbines and sabres – terrified to death – but not a cheer did they give to the noble women who beheld them from their doors – waveing to them their snow white handkerchiefs – weeping at the same time.

About 5 minutes after our *Rebs* had passed – the clattering of horses hoofs – ringing of sabres – and the loud "huzas" of the Yanks were heard – and in five minutes the town was swarming with them. Our "Post Commander" – had like a . . . – remained until the Yanks had entered town, then jumping his steed – he broke for life – and was hotly pursued – in the excitement of chase. He, the Post Commander – droped his *hat* and dismounted to regain it. The tale is told – he – and justly so – fell a captive for his *error* – to use a charitable term. The Yanks spread themselves – & I must say to their credit – were polite to the Ladies – kind and gentle to the Confederate wounded – and though two immense depots were stored with rations for our wounded – they would not molest a thing. By evening they had us all paroled and took their departure in a quiet manner – carrying off only a few of the able bodied Confederates – among whom was the gallant "Post Commander," who at the price of a hat – sold his temporary freedom – and services due his country. After the Yanks had been gone a half dozen hours – our gallant cavalry came *poking* up – ready for the *fray*.

By the last of September, the "Manassas Gap Railroad" had been repaired and transportation was by Rail from Warrenton to Richmond, via Culpeper Court House and Gordonsville, and a great many of the wounded had and were daily leaving on furlough. By the 3rd of Oct. I was able to mount my crutches and hobble about a little – and I immediately applied for a furlough. I was examined and refused – since the surgeons considered it dangerous for me even to leave my bed. I kept at them – and on the 6th myself and some 4 or 5 of my company were furloughed for 60 days to come to Texas. On the morning of Oct 7th myself – Sam Bailey – Sam Hughs[20] – and B. C. Simpson – all of Co. "A", started for Richmond – with furloughs in our pockets – Sam Bailey being the only one who was able to walk – the rest being packed on litters. Poor McMurtry – John Patton[21] – Dempsy being too bad off – were left with Norton – and all died – good and brave soldiers. I neglected to say that while in Warrenton – A. G. Monell[22] of our mess, passed through Warrenton on his way to the Company, having by reason of sickness been absent from "battle Manassas." Seeing myself and O'Mally both wounded – and Demsey Walker a corpse – he said – "Ah Bob – Fitzgerald is the only one of the Mess now in the Company – two wounded – and one dead – and myself absent, "ah" says he. "I would freely give this right arm of mine – had I but been with my old comrades" and bless his generous and patriotic soul. He deserted to the comforts of a private life a few months afterwards.

We took the cars on the 7th biding farewell to our kind Lady friends with sad grateful hearts and arrived in Richmond on the same evening – and were lodged at the "Institute Hospital" – where one of our Company – Jas. Farrell[23] was detailed as "Steward." We . . . good clean nice beds – in a comfortable room – and were fed well by our comrade, the said Farrell. We remained in this Hospital some three days – awaiting for our pay – passports and extension for 3 days of our furloughs. On the evening of the 3rd day they were placed in our hands – and myself and Sam Bailey – who was shot through the breast – started for Texas – each with a 60 day furlough.

Though possessed with a 60 day furlough, my time of return to the Army, independent of my wounds – was governed by my parole – given at Warrenton – "not to fight against the U.S. or do ought to their predjudice" until legally exchanged and no one could say when that exchange would take place.[24]

Sam Bailey and I – took the train about the 8th of Oct. – for Lynchburg – thence to Bristol – thence to Knoxville – thence to Atlanta [and] on to Montgomery where we held up for a rest for a few days – and here we met one of our young, Gaston Ash,[25] of the "Terry Rangers,"[26] also on furlough.

The day previous to our departure, Sam Bailey was taken with a chill – and though it was my desire to remain with him, he would not listen to the proposition, but urged myself and Gaston Ash to go on, that he would ketch up before we reached the Mississippi River. Biding our comrade good bye, we started for Mobile – when we safely arrived, and put up at the "Battle House" a fine and splendidly kept Hotel. Here Gaston Ash met his Lieut. Col. – Tom Harrison,[27] who was also on furlough – and as was well acquainted with my Father, was very glad to see me.

Here allow me to speak a word of praise in behalf of the noble Ladies who lived on the line of Rail Road from Richmond Va. – via Knoxville – to Montgomery Ala. Not a train passed a town, a station or "wooding up" place, but what dozens of Ladies, old and young, would rush aboard – followed by their servants bearing large baskets, groaning with the good things of life – and pitchers of milk, coffee and tea – to work they would go – feeding the poor Confederate – who was sick or wounded – dressing and binding his wounds. To them I feel grateful – since being on crutches, I was unable to navigate with any speed – consequently could not have got off the train for food. My wounds too were dressed. No soldier suffered – all were provided and cared for – by the noble and Christian women of the South. Would to God that every man, had been a woman in patriotism.

We stoped but a couple of days in Mobile – Gas. Ash, Col. Harrison and myself took the train for Meridian – then to Jackson, Miss. – where the Col. left us. We made no halt in Jackson, but moved on to *"Vicksburg"* the supposed Gibraltar of the South. At Vicksburg we remained several days – and all being quiet – no gunboats near, we took a good view of this already, and yet to be famous place. At V – we were joined by Joseph Cobb[28] – a gallant young soldier of the 6th Texas Cavalry – who was wounded in the head. Joe afterwards raised a Cavalry Company, and made a name – scouting on the Mississippi River, between Yazoo & Vicksburg. Joe – Ash and myself crossed the grand old Miss. River in a tug – hired a hack, which carried us some 12 miles from the river – to a point where we could take the "Vicksburg & Shrevesport RR" – the name of the place I do not now recollect. Arriving at this place – we found to our disgust that we would have to remain there several days. Swallowing our bad luck, we secured quarters in the family of a rich old planter – who kept a fine table – and by the by

– we here struck up with two more fellow travelers – and Texans too – who arrived the same day with ourselves, and were stoping with an adjoining planter. There were Mr. & Miss. Smith. Mr. S – was a young man – some 22 – & a member of 3 North Carolina Infantry – Virginia Army – though an adopted Texan – having joined a regiment of his native state – by being in NC when the war broke out. Miss. Smith was a young Lady, about 16 – and a most beautiful, amiable and interesting young Lady. She & Mr. S – were cousins. Her parents had moved to Texas and settled in Grimes Co. before the war, leaving her at school in NC. Her cousin was now bringing her out to Texas. *My heart was gone* – as well as Ash's and Cobb's – but for the moment, enough of the Smith biography. Here at this place, (confound the name, I disremember) I met up with one of my old Baton Rouge school mates – who was glad to see me. He gave a sorrowful tale concerning this section of the country – since the Yanks had made several raids – stole negroes and played the devil generally. Enough of this place – to my travels.

After being detained here a day or so – we paid our "bills" – and jumped aboard of the "locomotion train" and started for Monroe, Louisiana, some 60 miles distant. When within a few miles of Monroe – we were informed that the stage for Shrevesport La. would be in readiness to leave on the arrival of the cars – and well knowing that in these Confederate times that it was "Every man for himself and the devil for all," we knew that unless we were very quick and secured seats, we would have to wait in Monroe several days, so our party, composed of Mr. and Miss. Smith – Joe Cobb, Gaston Ash, and the "man on crutches," got together and held a consultation – and this conclusion was the result. Gaston Ash being lightfooted was ordered to jump from the cars and rush to a certain house, where we were informed that a *few* boarders would be taken. Joe Cobb – was ordered to rush to the station and secure seats, *if possible*. Mr. Smith – considering *all* circumstances was to take charge of Miss Smith – and myself – being unable to walk was left to follow Ash – who was to wave me on by a waveing candle. The cars reached Monroe about 10 P.M. – and as the cars were crowded – a general rush took place – each man following his own nose – our party followed their orders.

{ 87 }

Off Ash bounded then went Cobb – at a double quick – while *I,* seated upon a rail road tye, gazed upon the lovely Miss Smith as she gracefully moved off – hung to the arm of her confounded cousin. The house to which Ash was to go was not very far from the depot – and in a few moments, I saw the signal of success, and hobbled off to my intended retreat.

Arrived there – I was informed by Ash, "All right Bob – beds for us all, and supper cooking." The last news was welcome. Here I had the pleasure of seeing Genl. Jeff Thompson[29] – of Missouri fame – and was honored by an introduction – but old Jeff didn't say "won't you have a glass of rum" – for he was *bountifully* supplied. To me he looked more like a monkey than a man – but enough of this. We had hardly been in the house 15 minutes, before we heard the cry "Boys, oh Boys, come quick – stage leaves in a minute and I have got seats for us all" and here came bulging into the house old Joe Cobb. "Will we have time to finish our good landlords repast – for it will soon be ready, and I am damed hungry?" "Not a mouthful boys can you eat – or you will be left." "Is Miss Smith going on in the same stage Cobb?" quoth Ash. "You bet – I secured seats for her and that bumbled headed cousin myself!" That settled the question with Ash and myself – and down we stumbled for the stage stand, when we arrived in a few moments. "All aboard" cried the driver and in we jumped – and sure as life – there on the hind seat, sat the beautiful Miss S – her tow headed cousin – and a third party – whom I afterwards discovered to be a pious Baptist Lady. The driver cracked his whip – the 6 horse team snorted – and away we went for Shrevesport – 9 inside and a regiment on top.

In 36 hours we arrived safely at Shrevesport – where we were delayed a day. On [the] second day, the stage bugle blew – and we three of single bliss, being assured that Miss Smith would also go on in same stage – prepared to bid adieu to Shrevesport. By this time we had become very "thick" with Miss Sallies (Smith) cousin – to use a vulgarism. From Shrevesport we moved on to Marshall – one day from thence to Henderson – one night. Here a favorable chance made Miss Sallie and myself very good friends – for I had not as yet spoken to her. Nor was this chance at all owing to her "toe headed" cousin. The Baptist Lady left us at Henderson – and I took the liberty of occupying a rear seat – and another Lady passenger coming in, Mr. Harris was polite enough to "offer his hind seat" to said Lady passenger, which to my great joy she occupied. Soon striking up an acquaintance with Miss Sallie I had a most pleasant time the remainder of the trip. From Henderson we went to Rusk – 45 miles distant. On our arrival at Rusk, we found out that we would have to remain over a whole night. "If that is the case boys, let us have our fun" said Joe Cobb, who was wild and lively. Leaving me at the hotel – Cobb – Ash – and Smith started off up town – if such you can call the little place of Rusk. Being on crutches – I attracted a good deal of attention – as a maimed soldier was a "rare sight." Soon I had a large crowd of grey haired sires and youthful school boys on every side – asking a thousand and one questions about our Army – Genl. Lee – "Texas Brigade," battle Manassas, our prospects, and what I thought. Of course I spoke in a very confident way – telling them that the south was invincible and that our independence would soon be won. While thus making happy the hearts of the "reserve force" I discovered my three fellow travelers approaching the hotel – each with a big cake and three bottles of "champagne." "This way Bob" said Joe, as he gave me the wink – and after them I hobbled – leaving the impression upon the minds of my audience (judging from the whispers) that we "were a wild set." The boys repaired to our room in [the] 2nd story – when being joined by another "6th Texas cavalier." The "poping" of champagne corks soon began, and soon the whole crowd, excepting myself were in a "weaving way." In other words "3 sheets in the wind" alias tight. Here our young friend – Joe Cobb parted from us" and struck out for his home in Waco – another route from us. Up to this time, I was ignorant of the wherabouts of my Father and the family – having met one of my Brigade, Robt. Jarmon[30] at Vicksburg Msip. – on his return to Virginia from off furlough; he informed me that the yellow fever having broken out in Houston – and the Yanks taken Galveston, my Father had left Houston and removed, he knew not where. Here I met a gentleman, who knowing Pa told me that he was now living in Huntsville, Walker Co – directly on the route which I was now traveling and some 70 miles from Houston.

Remaining one night in Rusk, we started next morning for Crocket – Houston Co. – which place we reached in 18 hours journey – and where we were also detained a night. Leaving Crocket by 3 A.M. – we started for Huntsville where we were due – 5 P.M. On we went and by 4 1/2 P.M. we came in sight of Hunstville. What were my feelings? They cannot be explained. Eight months before, I had left home (in Houston) in fine health, sound in body, unaccustomed to the least suffering or hardship – but now how different. Maimed – perhaps for life – having been in some 4 bloody battles – suffered every conceivable hardship and misery – sun burnt – lousy – dirty – and clad in a coarse garb – a "grey Confederate uniform" – yet with all happy, and firm in my duty to my country.

Soon the bugle blew – and the way we went ratling down the streets of Huntsville – up to the "Huntsville Hotel" – where a large crowd of the two extreme of age were collected, to hear the "war news," from the stage passengers. As I was being helped from the stage a large portly gentleman – seemingly of 60 years – steped up to me and asked "Is this Judge Campbell's son" "Yes sir," replied I. "I am glad to see you Robt. – will show you your Fathers residence."

"Howdy Brother" said a couple of urchins as I turned around, and was grasped warmly by the hand, by my younger brothers. Biding adieu to my kind fellow travellers and my friend Miss Smith, I started to meet those who were dear to me. My little brothers shouldered my knapsack and I was hobbling away for the "paternal roof." After having gone some 500 yards – I cast my eye in my rear – and there beheld a train of some 30 "school boys" – whose love of glory and veneration for a wounded soldier made me conspicuous by attending me – more however from curiousity than ought else – and to satisfy them I had to pass down the line my "Confederate cap" with the ensignia of my regiment attached to it – then my crutch – my knapsack, & all the curiousities of a soldiers dress.

Arriving near a bountiful residence – with a large flower garden in front, it was pointed out to me as "our house." As I neared the gate – I saw my Father runing up the walk to meet me – with tears streaming down his eyes – then my Mother – and then my two sisters, and the toddling babe. "Thank God, my child, you are with us again," said my Father through his tears – as he threw his arms around me – and the tears of my Mother, the sweet kiss of affection from my sisters – the hearty shake of the hand from our faithful blacks – all told me that I was welcome home – and that prayers had been said for me while mid the dangers of the battlefield.

That scene shall *never* fade from my mind – while life lasts, since it was the most impressive to me. I now indeed felt a pride in the services I had rendered – since there were those who felt proud of me and what I had done.

Appendix A

LETTERS AND OTHER WRITINGS

Letter in the Houston Tri-Weekly Telegraph,
August 22, 1862

This excerpt of a letter Robert Campbell wrote to his father was printed in the *Houston Tri-Weekly Telegraph*, August 22, 1862, p. 2, col. 4. The letter is introduced by the newspaper editor.

Young Robert Campbell, of the Bayou City Guards, Co. A, 5th Texas, in a recent letter to his father, when speaking of the hard-fought and sanguinary battle of the 27th June, known as the affair of "Gaines' Mill," says:

In crossing the creek I got one foot bogged, and left my shoe, making the charge with one bare foot. Lieut. Clute made the charge with us unhurt. He had a large gray overcoat strapped on his back.

A few seconds before he was killed, he laughingly turned to the boys, saying: "Boys, I have got my ball in my coat" – a ball having gone into his coat and stopped there. I turned my head from him, and in less than ten seconds he was dead, a piece of shell having pased through him.

In another part of the same letter, he remarks:

We captured the 4th New Jersey – officers, colors, band and all. After their capture they exhibited great alarm. Some would approach our boys and say, "Please take care of me; we took care of your prisoners" – "Don't hurt me," &c. To one I gave the last chew of tobacco I had. I talked with several of the prisoners. One observed to me: "Boy, when do you think this war will end?" I replied, "When do you think you have a bigger job on hand than you can manage." He said, "You will then fight till your heads are grey." To that I remarked, "We intend to fight to the last." His observation was, "I glory in your spunk." Another prisoner said to me, "I am just in the fix I want to be." I wished to know of him if he had freely enlisted. His answer was, "No, I was very drunk; I was got in when in that state." Some of them would say, "Should you whip us, the war will end." They were very talkative, and now see that they are very much deceived by their Northern journals, and by their generals.

The same letter, in speaking of the capture of the 4th New Jersey, says:

With a whoop and a yell, the gallant 5th went at them – each of us, after firing, breaking for some fellow, and each took his own prisoner. I got hold of a big, strapping Dutchman, and ordered him to throw down his gun – he refused. I took aim at him and commanded him to surrender. He was in the act of raising his gun – I grasped it, dashed it down, and marched him off.

The Yanks whipped and the fight over, I was sent back three or four miles as a guard over prisoners, where we were relieved by Virginians. I went till morning without a shoe, when I got one – a few days before I had marched bare footed.

From the Yanks we got everything in the shape of clothing, edibles, and traps of various kinds. In them, however, I did not share, as I was sent back with prisoners, as I have already stated. He concludes by saying:

Thus ends my description of a bloody fight, in which the Texas Brigade distinguished itself, but paid dearly for the victory – the casualties reaching from 600 to 700 men,[1] but from which your son safely escaped, and for which I have thanked a kind and good God. I flatter myself that, though very young, and constantly and strongly temped, I am free from vice as when I left home. I never have left the regiment since I joined it at Yorktown. I get on well with all my companions, performing my duties as a soldier cheer-

fully, and to the best of my ability – at least, as well as any – for, to be candid, Texians can fight, but can't drill.

The Battle of Chickamauga

The following was pasted in Campbell's ledger. It was probably clipped from a Houston newspaper. Above the clipping, Campbell wrote this notation: "This is an extract taken from one of my letters to my Father after the battle of 'Chickamauga,' Georgia."

We take the following from a private letter from one of the Bayou City Guards.

Richmond, September 29th, 1863.
Before giving you an account of the battle of Chickamauga let me tell you of the trip we of Hood's Brigade took to reach the battle ground. We were quietly resting on the banks of the Rappahannock, Near Port Royal, when on the night of September 7th, orders came for us to be ready to move at 4 A.M., next day. Early on the morning of the 8th we left camp, and marched 12 miles to Milford Station, on the Fredericksburg Railroad. That night we took the cars to Richmond, where we arrived on the morning of the 9th. The same day we took the cars for Georgia, where we arrived after a trip of seven or eight days. Nothing of interest occurred on the trip except at every depot crowds of ladies were to be seen with flowers, refreshments, etc. At night bonfires were built along the railroad. Everybody appeared to be overflowing with patriotism.

We left the cars at Burnt Bridge, three miles from Ringgold, on the 17th, and the same evening received orders to prepare four day's rations. The next morning (18th) we were early on the march. We reached Ringgold at 9 A.M. Here General Forrest's[2] column joined us. At about 11 A.M., four miles from Ringgold, we flushed a lot of Yankees, and pursued them ten miles that day, Gen. Gregg's[3] Texans having a smart little brush with them in the evening. Our brigade did not exchange shots with the enemy that day, though we drove in their skirmishers in line of battle.

At 10 P.M. we lay down to rest, having thrown out our pickets. Early next morning we were aroused by reports of musketry, which told us that our skirmishers were at work. We formed in line and took our position in the fourth line of battle, where we rested till 2 P.M., except moving occasionally to keep from being flanked. Forrest brought on the fight that day by driving their skirmishers in. Walker's Division[4] went in about 10 A.M. and fought till about 12.

At 3 P.M., Gen. Law, who commanded a division, (Hood being in command of a corps) ordered us forward, and at it we went. We fired on them one or two rounds when first meeting them. But the ardor of the boys could not be restrained, so with a Texas

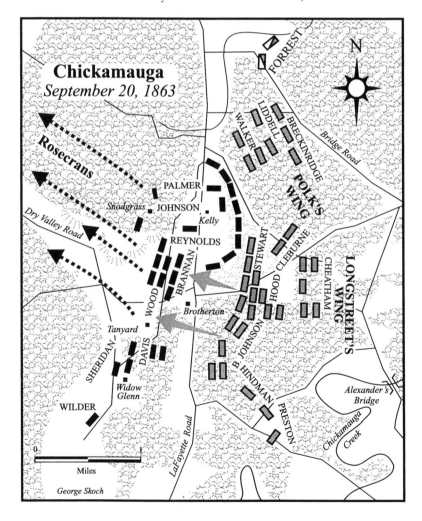

yell we went at them and drove them – run them like dogs – until our regiment, the Fifth, got so far ahead of the brigade, we had to fall back to prevent being flanked on both sides. Directly we heard a whoop, and saw the Yankees rushing upon us. We waited till they got within about a hundred yards of us, when with a jump and a yell, we rushed upon them. We drove them into a field, when a fresh line of battle coming on us, half the regiment stopped to shoot at them, while about 100 of us took after the running Yanks, and also made for a battery that was pouring a heavy fire upon us. We had got about half way to the battery when I was struck down by a minie, and had to leave the field.

Gen. Robertson fought nobly. Our opponents were Tennesseeans and Kentuckians. Our regiment was again in the action on Sunday, but as I was unable to see it, I will give you no account of the affair.

Yours truly,

Letter to Peter Gray, January 5, 1864

Robert Campbell wrote this letter after returning to his unit from furlough following his Chickamauga wound. The document is on file at the National Archives.

. . . Morristown East Tenn
January 5th 1864

Judge Peter W Gray

Dear Judge –
Hearing that you are in Richmond I have concluded to drop you a few lines on a small business matter of mine. When I came . . . last spring from home, I brought letters to you, Judge Oldham & Gen Wigfall from . . . & Gov Lubbock. also one from my father recommending me for promotion. Not Judge because I considered myself too good to serve as a private, but my wounds received at Manassas incapacitated me for further service in the infantry and I felt a delicacy in joining in a strange co. Besides my

father thought I should obtain a position I would be less exposed to the bad principles to which one is exposed in camp. Not, Dear Judge, that I am easily led astray, for I have no bad habits now, that I did not have before I joined the army – I neither gamble or drink – and I can say since I joined the army I have performed my duties as a soldier – as my officers can attest – neither have I stolen from others, which has become a manice in the army. I have been in six engagements – wounded twice at Manassas, once at Chickamauga. . . . still continue to come from my Manassas wound – and I am unfit for the duties of a soldier in the infantry or cavalry but I do . . . letters on to Judge Oldham asking him to aid me. I would like either to get a staff appointment or a commission to go to Texas & raise a Cavalry Co. – where the life of a soldier is not so active and where I believe I could stand it – & if these can not be obtained I wish Judge you would find out if the signal corps . . . & if so try & get me transfiard to it. To prove to you that I am incapacitated my Co commander said if I wanted he would discharge me. I told him no, never. I hope Judge you will aid me in this. If you would see Gen. Hood he might aid you. I hope Judge you will act as you think best for I regard you as a friend not only of my family but of myself & I am willing to follow your advice.

We are in Winter Qts. one mile from Morristown. To morrow I expect to start out with my regt as a guard for a forage train to be absent some two days.

Judge when you start to Texas I wish you would get from Mr. Boyles our agt at the depot a grey jacket of mine, which I had on when I was wounded. The . . . is all bloody and has the bullet hole in it. I want to send it home by you in just that fix.

Hoping Judge that you are in good health. I remain your young friend.

Robt Campbell
Co "A" 5th Texas Vols
Texas Brigade
Hood's Div

PS – Please write me soon and let me hear from you Judge.

Also on file at the National Archives is a portion of a letter written by the Honorable P. Gray on Campbell's behalf. The letter was dated January 21, 1864, and addressed "Mr. President." Gray introduces Campbell and summarizes his service record. He describes him as "a youth of excellent natural abilities & has received and profited by good instruction – and is of high morals and honorable principles." Added to the letter is a notation dated Richmond, January 23, 1864 – "I know him to be a gallant & good soldier. J. B. Hood, Maj Genl." Another notation, initialed "J.D.," directs the letter to the secretary of war for attention. Campbell was subsequently transferred to duty as a courier at brigade headquarters. He remained in that position until being furloughed due to wounds suffered in the battle at Darbytown Road on October 7, 1864.

"Gen. Lee at the 'Wilderness'"

This article, penned by "R.C., of Hood's Texas Brigade," was written after the war to describe events that occurred during the Battle of the Wilderness, May 5 – 6, 1864. The author describes himself as having been a courier on Brig. Gen. John Gregg's staff at the time of the battle. Evidence, though circumstantial, leads to the conclusion that Robert Campbell is "R.C." We know that Campbell was assigned as a courier at the headquarters of the Texas Brigade at the time of the battle.[5] He was one of five members of the brigade with the initials "R.C." to have survived the war (and thus be able to write the article) and the only one listed as having been assigned as a courier.[6] Campbell did use the initials "R.C." in place of signing his name at times. An example of this is found in one of the notes he wrote to explain a clipping he had pasted in the ledger book. Also, in his scrapbook Campbell added a note to a newspaper clipping of an account of the same event written by E. C. Wharton. In the note Campbell indicates his interest in the correct telling of this event by writing, "The foregoing, by Maj. E. C. Wharton of the New Orleans press, is in the main correct, but there are two or three errors that for my own pleasure, I shall here proceed to correct." Next to the note, Campbell pasted a letter he had written in response to a printed interview concerning casualty rates in which he describes his roll as a courier at the time of the "Lee to the rear" incident. He also remarks on the high casualty rate among the couriers, claiming he was the only one not killed or wounded except for two who had been sent off to have ordnance brought up. The following appeared in *The Land We Love,* October 1868, pp. 481 – 86.

In reading the February number of "The Land We Love," your correspondent read with unfeigned pleasure the able article under head of *"The Lost Dispatch,"* which was a partial criticism upon E. A. Pollard's "Lost Cause"[7] – a work that assumes the glorious task of recording truthfully the deeds and experience of Confederate arms, but which, in fact, prostitutes its pages to abuse of our late President, and in giving incorrect, unfair and impartial statements of both actors and their acting. In "The Lost Dispatch" the position is well taken that the *true* history of our late struggle will be the labor of that historian, who dilligently collects from every source possible, the information oral and written which those who were actors are able to give, and upon this data of fact build, in an honest and impartial manner, the glorious historical structure which is to tell the future ages and generations of the gallant struggle which the Southern people made for their liberty and independence. From the Field Marshal to the humblest private in the ranks, each has a rich store of information – and as a thousand mountain rills go to form the deep and fast rolling waters of a majestic river – so will these varied and multifarious sources, from whence will flow the correct history of our late war, have to be consulted before truth can place her seal upon any writing that assumes to be a history of the Confederate States upon land and upon sea.

An humble participant in the late war, I take upon myself the liberty of seeking in your columns a brief space for the purpose of mentioning and preserving from error, an important incident of the late contest – which deserves to occupy one of the brightest pages upon our country's history. I come prepared to state what I saw and what I heard, and not what was reported to me through many mouths – I shall be brief – for were my pen able, no ornamentation from it, could add to the glory and grandeur of the main fact that I shall state.

That Gen. R. E. Lee exposed his life during the battle of the "Wilderness," May 6, 1864, is generally known to the Southern people – but the truth of the affair has never, to my knowledge, been given – I have read accounts, both in prose and poetry, of Gen. Lee's noble conduct on the eventful 6th of May – but however near to the truth of the case – and were written, perhaps, by some who "snuffed the battle from afar," and gathered their records from those who fled in the face of danger – the truth is this.

In the fall of 1863, Gen. Longstreet, with two divisions of his corps (Hood's and McLaw's[8]) was ordered to Georgia to reinforce Gen. Bragg.[9] This we did, and participated in the battle of "Chickamauga," after which we were ordered to Knoxville, Tennessee to lay siege to the place, and which was done without success.

In the latter part of April, 1864, Gen. Longstreet found himself and corps in the vicinity of Bristol, on the Virginia and Tennessee line. About May 1st, 1864, we took up the line of March, and were transported to Cobham station, on the Virginia Central Railroad, near Charlottesville. At this place new clothing, guns, bayonets, ammunition and ample provisions were issued to our corps, and we were reviewed by Generals Lee and Longstreet. At that time our corps contained only the two divisions that Longstreet took with him to Georgia. During our stay in Georgia and Tennessee, Gen. Hood was made a Lieutenant General, and Major Gen. Field[10] assigned in his place. Maj. Gen. McLaws was removed and Brig. Gen. Kershaw,[11] of South Carolina, made a Major General in his stead, and my old brigade, "Texas," was placed under Brig. Gen. Jno. Gregg, of Texas – vice Brig. Gen. Robertson removed.

We took up the line of march from Cobham station about the 2nd or 3rd of May – which, I now forget – and continued on a steady march until the night of the 5th, going into camp about 7 or 8 P.M. Late in the evening of the 5th we heard the report of cannon, and were informed that we were near Gen. Lee's army. We did not know at the time that the grand battle of the "Wilderness" had begun on the 5th, and merely deemed the report of cannon "a feeling of the enemy's position." At this time, as I had been for several months, I was acting on Gen. Gregg's staff as courier – and in a position to see and know all that I have, or may hereafter relate.

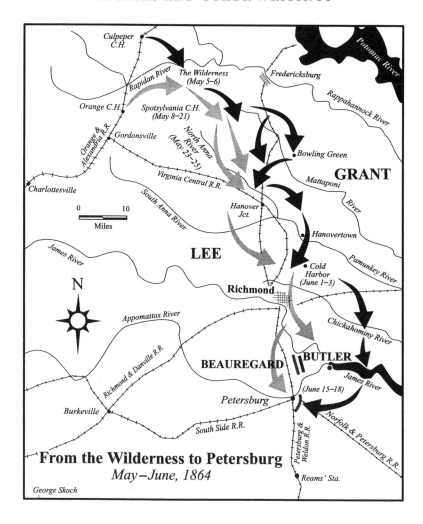

From the Wilderness to Petersburg
May–June, 1864

George Skoch

By 3 A.M., on the morning of the 6th, the long roll beat, the men were aroused, under arms, and the march soon began. We moved steadily on, though rather at a rapid pace, with the "Texas Brigade" leading the van of Gen. Field's division. By daylight, or perhaps a little later, we had reached the turnpike known as the "Fredericksburg Turnpike." By daylight the boom of cannon, and the distant rattle of small arms, were borne upon the breeze, and knowing that the two armies were immediately facing each other, we recognized that a grand battle had begun, and we would soon be called upon to act well our part. Reaching the turnpike, we took the direction leading to Fredericksburg, and before going very far not only was our speed accelerated, but Gen. Kershaw's division (the other division of our corps) occupied the pike side and side with us, and thus situated, the two divisions moved rapidly in the direction of the firing – the men of separate commands mingling one with another.

When moving down this pike, the sun rose beautifully, but to the notice of all had a deep, red color, and the brave Gen. Gregg, upon seeing this, remarked to those who were riding near him, "there is the sun of Austerlitz"[12] – a prophecy that found verification ere it sunk to rest among the somber shades of night. The nearer our steps led us towards the firing, the din of battle became louder and more terrible. Faster and faster our columns moved on to the scene of conflict, until we were almost at a double-quick. Directly horsemen came dashing to and fro; aids were cantering about; ambulances containing the wounded went flying to the rear; litters with their unfortunate burdens were moving towards the hospitals; stragglers without number were flocking back with tales of distress, annihilation and defeat – all these signs betokened that bloody and desperate work was going on, and that too not many yards distant. A half mile more, and by 6 o'clock, we found ourselves upon the scene. Both of our divisions mingled together in one mass upon the turnpike. As a part of this narative, I will give the situation of affairs as we found them upon our arrival at the scene, and a short or imperfect idea of the ground.

The position where we found ourselves upon being halted, was near the brink of a hill which gradually sloped down for the distance of 200 yards, where immediately began the dense undergrowth known as the wilderness. The turnpike led over and down this hill and continued on into the wilderness. Immediately at the turn of the hill, where the turnpike or plank-road passed, hasty breastworks were partially constructed and under construction; and along these were strewn a body of stragglers that had been rallied, as well as some half dozen pieces of artillery that were playing upon the dense wilderness below. Near this hasty defense we found, upon our arrival, our loved commander-in-chief, Gen. Lee, Gen. Longstreet, their staffs, and bodyguards. I have often seen Gen. Lee, but never did I see him so excited, so disturbed – never did anxiety or care manifest itself before so plainly upon his countenance. If I mistake not he was almost moved to tears – if in error, others share it with me, and his voice was anxious and tremulous. And well, kind reader, may his anxiety have been great. The evening before, Gen. A. P. Hill, with divisions of Generals Wilcox[13] and Heath,[14] had met the enemy upon the ground before us, and night found them victorious. That night, (May 5th,) supposing the enemy demoralized and fleeing, they placed their pickets but a stone's throw in advance of the line of battle, and laid aside their accoutrements and arms, at least such is my latter day information. But be this as it may, they were attacked next morning, at break of day, unawares, and unprepared, and ere many blows were struck, the great body of Gen. Hill's two divisions were in full flight – and an overwhelming and victorious enemy had only a handful of brave souls who dared stay their advance. On they came, and by 6 or 7 A.M., at which time our corps (Longstreet's) came upon the scene, the enemy were not far from the hill before described – and unless checked would soon possess it, be out of the wilderness, and prepared to strike us a death blow. The other division of Gen. Hill's corps, (Gen. Anderson's),[15] for some reason, had not arrived as soon as was expected. Here let me say that if in aught written I have done any injustice to the brave men who composed Gen. Hill's corps, it is not so intended. That their conduct on that day was natural from the circumstances, we cannot deny. I will also state here, that since that battle, I have learned that when our corps set out that morning, (May 6th,) at 3 A.M., we were on a flank movement, and that Gen. Hill being attacked and routed, the flank movement was abandoned in order that this position might be relieved.

As we stood upon this hill, Lee excited and in close consultation with Longstreet – our batteries thundering into the Wilderness below, the roar of musketry from the undergrowth below – our men retreating in a disorganized mass, and the Yankees pressing on and within musket shot, almost, of the hill upon which stood our idolized chief, indeed was an exciting time, and the emergency called for *immediate* and *determined* action upon the part of the Confederate General. Lee was equal to the hour. Action must *not* be delayed, for in less than five minutes the enemy would be upon the hill. Longstreet's corps as it then stood in one mingled mass upon the plank road, could not be thrown in, and time must be allowed for it to reform, and place itself in line of battle. The cannon thundered, musketry rolled, stragglers were fleeing, couriers riding here and there in post-haste, minnies began to sing, the dying and wounded were jolted by the flying ambulances, and filling the road-side, adding to the excitement the terror of death. The "Texas Brigade," was in front of Field's division – while "Humphrey's brigade"[16] of Mississippians led the van of Kershaw's division. The consultation ended. Gen. Gregg and Gen. Humphrey were ordered to form their brigades in line of battle, which was quickly done, and we found ourselves near the brow of the hill, Gregg on the left – Humphrey on the right. "Gen. Gregg prepare to move," was the order from Gen. L. About this time, Gen. Lee, with his staff, rode up to Gen. Gregg – "General what brigade is this?" said Lee. "The Texas Brigade," was General G's. reply. "I am glad to see it," said Lee. "When you go in there, I wish you to give those men the cold steel – they will stand and fire all day, and never move unless you charge them." "That is my experience," replied the brave Gregg. By this time an aid from General Longstreet rode up and repeated the order, "advance your command, Gen. Gregg." And now comes the point upon which the interest of this "o'er true tale" hangs. *Attention Texas Brigade*" was rung upon the morning air, by Gen. Gregg, *"the eyes of General Lee are upon you, forward, march."* Scarce had we moved a step, when Gen. Lee, in front of the whole command, raised himself in his stirrups, uncovered his grey hairs, and with an earnest, yet anxious voice, exclaimed above the din and confusion of the hour, *"Texans always move them."* Reader, for near four years I followed the fortunes of the Virginia army, heard, saw and experienced much that saddened the heart or appealed in one form or another to human passions, but never before in my lifetime or since, did I ever witness such a scene as was enacted when Lee pronounced these words, with the appealing look that he gave. A yell rent the air that must have been heard for miles around, and but a few eyes in that old brigade of veterans and heroes of many a bloody field was undimmed by honest, heartfelt tears. Leonard Gee,[17] a courier to Gen. Gregg, and riding by my side, with tears coursing down his cheeks and yells issuing from his throat exclaimed, "I would charge hell itself for that old man." It was not what Gen. Lee said that so infused and excited the men, as his tone and look, which each one of us knew were born of the dangers of the hour.

With yell after yell we moved forward, passed the brow of the hill, and moved down the declivity towards the undergrowth – a distance in all not exceeding 200 yards. After moving over half the ground we all saw that Gen. Lee was following us into battle – care and anxiety upon his countenance – refusing to come back at the request and advice of his staff. If I recollect correctly, the

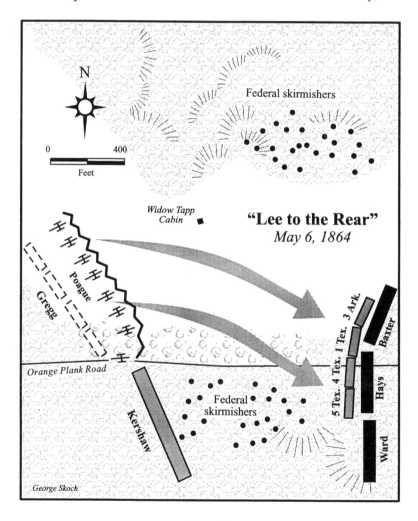

brigade halted when they discovered Gen. Lee's intention, and all eyes were turned upon him. Five and six of his staff would gather around him, seize him, his arms, his horse's reins, but he shook them off and moved forward. Thus did he continue until just before we reached the undergrowth, not, however, until the balls began to fill and whistle through the air. Seeing that we would do all that men could do to retrieve the misfortunes of the hour, accepting the advice of his staff, and hearkening to the protest of his advancing soldiers, he at last turned round and rode back to a position on the hill.

We reached the undergrowth – entered it with a yell, and in less than 100 yards came face to face with the advancing, triumphant, and sanguine foe – confronted only by a few brave souls who could only fire and yield their ground. The enemy were at least five or six to one of us, and death seemed to be our portion. With only 15 or 20 paces separating us, the contest waxed hotter and deadlier. We gave a cheer and tried a charge, but with our handful of men our only success was to rush up to them, shoot them down, and shove them back some 10 to 15 yards. For 25 minutes we held them steady – not a foot did they advance, and at the expiration of that time more than half of our brave fellows lay around us dead, dying and wounded, and the few survivors could stand it no longer. By order of Gen. Gregg, whose manly form was seen wherever danger gloried most – I bore the order to the 5th and 1st Texas, to fall back in order.

After retreating some 50 yards, a most deafening yell was borne upon the breeze, and ere we were prepared to realize its cause, Gen. Longstreet's corps came sweeping by us, reformed, and reinforced by Gen. Anderson's division, and with a valor that stands unrivaled swept everything before them for three long miles – driving, in that long charge, the yankees from four different lines of breastworks that they had thrown up in their rear. The "Battle of the Wilderness" was won – all other fighting by the enemy that day and the next was to prevent defeat from terminating in destruction.

The object, reader, of the advance made by Gregg and Humphrey, was to hold the enemy in check, to give Longstreet time to reform his corps. We accomplished our objective.

The "Texas Brigade" entered the fight 673 strong. We lost, in killed and wounded over 450.[18] Did we or did we not do all that men could? Gen. Gregg entered the fight with at least 12 commissioned and non-commissioned on his staff. Of these, several were killed, some wounded, and only two horses untouched. Gen. G's. horse was pierced by 5 balls – each creating a mortal wound – though he rode him until we fell back – sent him to the rear where he died.

My task is finished – and I have only to say if there ever lived a brave, fearless, unflinching and noble soldier – if ever there breathed a pure and honest patriot, he is to be found in that mouldering dust of a certain coffin in Hollywood cemetery, which contains the remains of Brig. Gen. Jno. Gregg, who fell near Richmond, Va., Oct. 7th. 1864, one of the best, the truest, the noblest men that Texas ever claimed.

Letter to Houston Telegraph, *August 13, 1864*

The following is a newspaper clipping preserved in Robert Campbell's ledger. Above the clipping is a handwritten notation: "This letter was written by me during the 'War' at which time I was an occasional corrospondent of 'Houston Telegraph' paper, under nom de plume of 'Stonewall.' It is the only one preserved." The number of men available for duty that Campbell gives at the end of the letter seems low. Company A (Bayou City Guards) had twenty-nine men listed on its muster roll dated August, 1864.[19] He may have been counting only men able to report for duty, omitting those ill but on the roster.

Camp "Texas Brigade" Chafins' Farm
August 13th, 1864

Editor Telegraph: – In my last to you I promised to write should anything of importance transpire. Many things have transpired, bloody battles have been fought, victories have been won, disasters have been sustained, and yet I have failed to write. Yet it is well known that our means of communication with Texas are quite limited.

Ere this you have doubtless had full particulars of the battles of the "Wilderness" and "Spotsylvania Court House," hence I will enter into no special details. This corps was ordered to Tennessee the first of last September, where it arrived in time to participate in the battle of "Chickamauga" and aid in defeating Rosencranz.[20] We remained near Chattanooga until about the first of November, when we were ordered by Gen. Bragg to march against Knoxville. We met the Yanks under Burnside[21] at Louden, and drove them into the city of Knoxville. Longstreet laid seige to Knoxville, and would have eventually taken it, but as usual Gen. Bragg was defeated by Grant[22] at Chattanooga, compelling Longstreet to fall back, as Grant as soon as he had defeated Bragg, cut off our communication with Bragg and our base, and also sent a large force to aid Burnside. We were compelled to fall back, which we did with the least loss. Retreated as far as Rogersville. We then advanced to Morristown, where we built winter quarters. After remaining in them about two weeks we were marched down on Frenchbroad river about two miles from Knoxville, and the rest of the winter (which was nearly all) we were marching and campaigning in rain, snow and cold.

The men, a large portion *entirely* barefooted, and as for clothes, the whole command was nearly destitute; their clothes being in rags, kept on them by tying together with strings, the government having failed to furnish us with any clothing at all for six or eight months. We were not fed with any too much, either, though we did better in that line than any other. The government certainly did treat this command shamefully. About the middle of April we moved from "Russelville" (about 14 miles from Knoxville) for Zollicoffer, where, after remaining some two weeks, we took the cars for old Virginia, and by the 1st of May we were prepared for battle under our old chieftain, Gen. Lee. On the 6th of May the "Texas Brigade" fought in her usual gallant style, complimented by Gen. Lee with the remark, "Texians always move thus." He endeavored to follow us into the fight but was held back by his staff. What I relate I *heard* and *saw*. At Spotsylvania Court House we again struck for Texas; and though the Yanks did get into the trench of the Brigade, they found men, for our boys took it hand to hand. The Yanks used the bayonet very freely among the 1st Texas. We, after a half hour's hand to hand fight, drove them out, leaving their dead piled in our trenches. After being defeated at Spotsylvania, Grant made another flank movement to the left. Lee confronted him at Hanover Junction. Grant refused to fight, but flanked again to the left and confronted us in McClellan's old position. He butted at our breastworks a time or two, near Coal [Cold] Harbor, but could not move us, his loss being *very heavy.*

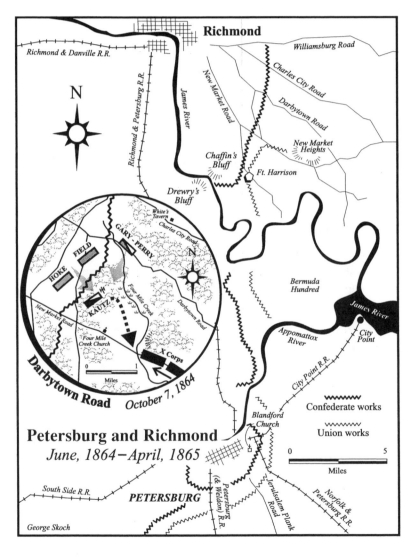

The Texas Brigade was partially engaged. Grant flanked again to his left, with a little more success than before. He succeeded in getting a large force near Petersburg and capturing some of our batteries and a portion of the breastworks right at Petersburg before Gen. Lee could reinforce Beauregard.[23] Petersburg was certainly in imminent danger before Lee arrived as Beauregard had fought his small band against nearly half the Yankee army; but Lee arrived in time to turn the tables, and Petersburg remains unconquered. Grant laid siege to Petersburg, abandoning the north side of the James River entirely. He endeavored to break our communication with the south by cutting the Weldon railroad, also the Petersburg and Danville railroad, but in this he lost five to ten thousand men in killed, wounded and captured, besides being driven back in confusion. Since then he threw near thirty thousand Yanks this (north) side James River, and made a heavy demonstration, thereby hoping Lee would be deceived. Lee was too sharp for him: he took from Petersburg enough troops (this division among others) to repulse 30,000 Yanks. As soon as we arrived, Grant took the back track for Petersburg, and . . . , but Lee moved back to Petersburg as soon as Grant, moving Field's Division here. As soon as the mine[24] had been sprung the Yanks raised a mighty shout, and charged, pouring in overwhelming numbers into the excavation made by the explosion, the negro troops leading the charge, crying "No quarter, remember Fort Pillow,"[25] and report says our boys did remember Fort Pillow, for they, like Gen. Forrest, killed nearly all the negroes.

The Yanks were driven back after they had taken our breastworks, gaining in the end not [an] inch of ground, paying for the frolic near 6000 men, our loss being about twelve hundred. Since then U. S. Grant has kept very quiet. I suppose he is awaiting operations in Georgia. Gen. Early has been near enough Washington to serenade "Old Abe" with the tune of Dixie.[26] We all have confidence in our success. We believe that God is with us, and hope ere long to be able to return to our Texas homes.

All of the "Bayou Guards" are well and cheerful, having about eight men present for duty. Our regiments are small, the three Texas regiments numbering about one hundred and ten men fit for duty.

You may expect to hear from me again, should important events transpire in this department. Lieut. Gen. Pemberton[27] has resigned, and now occupies the position of Lieut. Col. of artillery, and has charge of the artillery near Richmond. "STONEWALL"

Request for Payment of Claim

In Robert Campbell's file in the National Archives are a series of letters written concerning a claim for payment owed to Campbell for the loss of his horse, killed at the battle of Fort Harrison. The horse had been appraised when it entered the service, but the original appraisal was lost. Finally satisfied as to the merits of the claim, the Confederate government awarded Campbell payment for the horse. In the meantime, Campbell had once again been wounded, this time at Darbytown Road. He wrote the following letter shortly after being furloughed. It was witnessed by Lt. Col. King Bryan[28] of the 5th Texas and B. P. Fuller, a lieutenant in Campbell's company. Capt. John Shotwell[29] had been on the brigade staff at the same time as Campbell.

Richmond, Va

Nov 12th 64

This is to certify that I empower Capt. John Shotwell Co "B" 1st Texas to draw one thousand ($1000.00) dollars due me by Confederate States for horse killed in action at Ft Harrison, Sept. 29th 1864.

Robt Campbell

Co "A" 5th Texas Vols

Witness

K Bryan

B. P. Fuller

Letter to Houston Weekly Telegraph, *January 20, 1865*

This letter was written by Campbell from his Huntsville, Texas, home while on leave from the army. At the time of the Civil War, newspapers mined the pages of papers from other cities as a primary source of news to print – thus Campbell's reference to the newspapers he was sending with the letter. Campbell's rather rosy description of conditions in Virginia may have been meant to boost morale at home; in Richmond the supply situation had become desperate.[30] The newspaper editor's introduction to the letter is included. From the *Houston Weekly Telegraph*, January 20, 1865, p. 4, col. 2.

    We have just received the following cheering note from our friend Robert Campbell, son of Hon. R. C. Campbell, of Huntsville:

                        Huntsville, Texas, Jan 17, 1865.
    Editor Telegraph: – I have just arrived home on furlough, suffering from a wound received on Oct. 7th, in the battle of Darbytown, Va., through the right lung and in left knee. I send you a few papers, which have been some time on the way, consequently they are old – though you may find some interesting local items. Our army in Virginia is in the best of spirits, well clad and fed, better than ever before, and is increasing. States are sending on conscripts and wagons, and clerks are being put into the ranks, and their places filled by negroes and disabled soldiers. All of the "Bayou City Guards" were well, that is, all that are left. The Texas Brigade is not much larger than a corporal's guard,[31] though still unconquered.

                              Your obedient servant,
                                Robert Campbell
                            Company A, 5th Texas.

Request for Medical Discharge

This letter was pasted in Campbell's ledger book. In an accompanying note, Campbell explains that his goal was not to escape service but that his wounds made it very difficult to serve in the field, especially in a cold climate. He hoped that if he was released from service, he would be able to form his own command. The board's decision, given in a letter dated April 5, 1865, and also pasted in the ledger book, was to recommend Campbell for service in the cavalry. A handwritten letter in the scrapbook contains orders from a Confederate command in Texas directing him to raise a mounted unit. Campbell notes that the end of the war prevented execution of that order.

Houston, Texas
April 4th, 1865

Col Thos M. Jack[32]

  Sir

  I have the honor to ask permission to appear before the "Medical Examining Board" at Houston for "Retirement." My wounds received in the Confederate Service have rendered me unfit for Field Duty. At 2nd Battle of Manassas, I was shot through the right leg – at Chickamauga, through the arm – at Darby Town, Va. through the lungs.

I am Col Very Respectfully
Your Obt Srvt
Robt Campbell
Co "A" 5th Texas Inf.

Appendix B

MUSTER ROLL ENTRIES

FOR ROBERT CAMPBELL

ENLISTED: WHEN: March 14, 1862
TO WHAT TIME: duration of the war
BY WHOM: Lt. J. E. Clute
WHERE: Houston, Texas
MUSTER-IN: Near Gordontown, Virginia, April 24, 1862
(muster-in to date to March 14, 1862)

Muster Roll Period	Present/Absent	Remarks
March & April, 1862	Present	
May & June, 1862	Present	
July & August, 1862	Absent	Wounded at Manassas, August 30, 1862. Sent to hospital.
September & October, 1862	Absent	(same as above) Taken prisoner and paroled at Warrenton, Virginia, September 29, 1862. Furloughed October 23, 1862.

November & December, 1862	Absent	(same as above) On furlough in Texas
January & February, 1863	Absent	(same as above)
March & April, 1863	Absent	(same as above)
May & June, 1863	Absent	On furlough for 60 days, dated from June 2, 1863
July & August, 1863	Present	
September & October, 1863	Absent	Wounded at Chickamauga, Georgia, September 19, 1863. On furlough in Virginia.
November & December, 1863	Present	Furloughed to Selma, Alabama, 40 days from November 4, 1863
January & February, 1864	Present	Detailed as courier at Brigade Headquarters, February 27, 1864
March & April, 1864	Present	(same as above)
May & June, 1864	Present	(same as above, except dated from February 2, 1864)
July & August, 1864	Present	(same as above)
September & October, 186	Absent	Wounded since October 7, 1864
November & December, 1864	Absent	(same as above) Furloughed November 8, 1864 – 60 days.
April 9, 1865	Absent	Furloughed in Texas.

Sources: Muster rolls of Company A, 5th Texas Infantry, C.S.A., with additional information from hospital registers and other records of detached service, all located in the National Archives, Washington, D.C.

NOTES

Introduction

1. Unidentified newspaper obituary clipping, undated, Campbell scrapbook.

2. Petersburg Railroad pass, dated November 4, 1863, issued by the C.S.A. War Department, Campbell ledger book.

3. For a history of the Bayou City Guards, with a focus on its individual members, see James Orville Moore, "The Men of the Bayou City Guards (Company A, 5th Texas Infantry, Hood's Brigade)." A detailed history of the Texas Brigade is found in Harold B. Simpson, *Hoods' Texas Brigade: Lee's Grenadier Guard.*

4. Martin L. Callahan, "Returned with Honor: The Flag of the 5th Texas," *North South Trader's Civil War* 25, no. 2 (Mar. – Apr., 1998): 36 – 42; *Marlin (Tex.) Daily Democrat*, June 26, 1903; *Houston Chronicle*, June 25, 1924.

5. *Houston Tri-weekly Telegraph*, Feb. 28, 1865, p. 7; Alan K. Sumrall, *Battle Flags of Texans in the Confederacy*, p. 19.

6. *Houston Weekly Telegraph*, Mar. 7, 1865, p. 2.

7. Campbell's assignments are documented in his muster-roll and hospital-register records on file at the National Archives.

8. The letter is part of Robert Campbell's military records file at the National Archives.

9. Eddy R. Parker, ed., *Touched by Fire: Letters from Company D, 5th Texas Infantry, Hood's Brigade, Army of Northern Virginia, 1862–1865*, p. 97. The letter was written by Mark Smither to his sister.

10. Several of Robert Campbell's obituaries clipped from newspapers are in the scrapbook. None were labeled with identification. They range in length from several paragraphs to a single paragraph. More than one seem to be from Yazoo City newspapers, while others seem to be from other communities in which Campbell had lived or had contacts.

11. Reilly's North Carolina Artillery was officially known as Company D, 1st North Carolina Artillery Regiment and was also known as the Rowan Artillery for their home in Rowan County, North Carolina. During the time the battery was associated with the Texas Brigade, they

were commanded by Capt. James Reilly. Harold B. Simpson, *Hood's Texas Brigade: A Compendium*, pp. 455 – 56.

12. Ibid., p. 3; Robert M. Powell, *Recollections of a Texas Colonel at Gettysburg*, ed. Gregory A. Coco, pp. 3 – 5, 36.

Chapter 1

1. The first Texas troops to go to war in Virginia went on their own as independent companies late in the spring of 1861. They would become the 1st Texas Infantry. On June 30, 1861, Confederate president Jefferson Davis called for troops from the various states to serve in the Confederate army. The Texas contribution to this call for troops was twenty companies, or approximately two thousand men. They traveled to Virginia in the late summer and early fall of 1861. In September of that year they were designated the 4th and 5th Regiments of Texas Infantry. (The 2d and 3d Texas Infantry had already been formed back in Texas.) They were brigaded with the 1st Texas, Brig. Gen. Louis T. Wigfall commanding. At this point in the war, the army had not yet been given the name it would make famous – "The Army of Northern Virginia."

2. The Battle of Eltham's Landing, on May 7, 1862, was the first full-scale combat for the Texans. Appomattox Court House was the scene of their final surrender on April 9, 1865.

3. James J. Archer was born at Bel Air, Maryland, on December 19, 1817. A lawyer at the time of the Mexican War, Archer volunteered and received a captain's commission. In 1855 he reenlisted and again served as a captain. Archer resigned his commission when the Civil War broke out. He joined the Confederate army and on October 2, 1862, was appointed colonel of the 5th Texas. When Brig. Gen. Louis Wigfall resigned his commission, Archer replaced him in command of the Texas Brigade, but a month later command of the brigade was given to a West Point graduate, John Bell Hood. Commanding a Tennessee brigade, Archer was captured at Gettysburg, and imprisoned at Johnson's Island, Ohio, until the summer of 1864, when he was exchanged. Archer died on October 24, 1864, in Richmond. William C. Davis, ed., *The Confederate General*, vol. 1, pp. 36 – 39.

4. Jerome B. Robertson had been elected captain of the company he raised in Texas on August 3, 1861. That unit became Company I, 5th Texas Infantry. Robertson was promoted to lieutenant colonel on October 10, 1861, and to colonel on June 2, 1862. Commanding the regiment, Robertson was wounded at Gaines's Mill on June 27, 1862, and again at Second Manassas on August 30, 1862. He was assigned command of the Texas Brigade on October 22, 1862, and promoted to brigadier general ten days later. Robertson again was wounded at Gettysburg. On February 25, 1864, he was court-martialed after a political dispute with Brig. Gen. Micah Jenkins and Lt. Gen. James Longstreet. Afterward, Robertson was sent west to the Trans-Mississippi Department and finished the war in Texas. Jerome B. Robertson,

comp., *Touched with Valor: Civil War Papers and Casualty Reports of Hood's Texas Brigade,* ed. Harold B. Simpson, pp. 11 – 17.

5. Walter Browne Botts (also referred to in the literature as Brown W. Botts) was a Virginia-born lawyer and the original captain of Company A, 5th Texas, Campbell's company. He was promoted within the regiment to major on November 4, 1861, and to lieutenant colonel on June 1, 1862. Botts resigned his commission due to "shattered health" and returned to Texas on July 17, 1862. He died in 1894. Robert K. Krick, *Lee's Colonels: A Biographical Register of the Field Officers of the Army of Northern Virginia,* p. 63.

6. Campbell is referring to John W. Kerr, the original second lieutenant of Company I, 5th Texas, from Washington County. He was promoted to first lieutenant on October 23, 1861, and appointed adjutant for the regiment on August 1, 1862, succeeding William Sellers, who had been made adjutant in October, 1861. Kerr was appointed acting assistant brigade adjutant on October 22, 1862. He was promoted to captain on November 2, 1863, and to brigade inspector general on December 3, 1863. Kerr was paroled with the brigade at Appomattox on April 12, 1865. Harold B. Simpson, *Hood's Texas Brigade: A Compendium,* p. 5.

7. John Bell Hood was a Kentuckian by birth. A West Point graduate, he was stationed in California and Texas before the war. After leading the 4th Texas, Hood was given command of the brigade in March, 1862, and promoted to command of the division prior to the march into Maryland that September. He later attained command of a corps and then the Army of Tennessee. But Hood was overmatched at these levels, and his service was marked by failure. As a regimental, brigade, and division commander, though, Hood was heroically successful, and the brigade he commanded retained his name, in tribute to him, even after Hood had moved to higher command. Richard M. McMurry, *John Bell Hood and the War for Southern Independence.*

8. John Marshall was born in Virginia. He moved to Mississippi during his youth and then relocated to Texas in 1854. Before the war Marshall worked as a journalist. He was appointed lieutenant colonel of the 4th Texas on October 2, 1861. He was promoted to colonel on March 3, 1862. Marshall was killed at Gaines's Mill on June 27, 1862. Krick, *Lee's Colonels,* p. 263.

9. Virginia-born Bradfute Warwick studied medicine before the war. He was appointed major of the 4th Texas on October 2, 1861. He was later promoted to lieutenant colonel. On June 27, 1862, Warwick was wounded at Gaines's Mill. He died of the wound on July 6, 1862, and was posthumously promoted to colonel. Ibid., pp. 387 – 88.

10. Louis T. Wigfall was born on April 21, 1816, in Edgefield, South Carolina. He took up the practice of law and in 1846 moved to Texas. Wigfall became the first commander of the Texas Brigade. He proved to be a bombastic general, easily startled. That trait resulted in his troops being roused in the middle of the night to defend against imaginary attackers. The Texan's did not mourn Wigfall's departure when he resigned his commission to take a position in the Confederate con-

gress. There he became a constant and vocal critic of Pres. Jefferson Davis. Alvy L. King, *Louis T. Wigfall, Southern Fire-eater;* Simpson, *Hood's Texas Brigade: Lee's Grenadier Guard,* pp. 70 – 89.

11. John C. G. Key was born in South Carolina in 1809 and practiced law in Louisiana and Texas before the war. He was the original captain of Company A, 4th Texas. Key was promoted to major on March 3, 1862. Soon after promotion to lieutenant colonel, he was wounded at Gaines's Mill on June 27,and promoted to colonel in July. Key was wounded again at Gettysburg and retired due to ill health on April 29, 1864. He died in 1866. Krick, *Lee's Colonels,* p. 222.

12. Thomas Overton Moore was a sugar planter who served in both houses of the Louisiana legislature before being elected governor in November, 1860. A staunch supporter of the Confederacy, Moore quickly began supplying the army with material and troops. During the war, he banned the export of cotton, hoping to influence foreign powers to support the South. At the end of the war, the state legislature ordered Moore's arrest. He fled to Cuba but was later pardoned and returned to his plantation. Stewart Sifakis. *Who Was Who in the Confederacy,* p. 203.

13. J. E. Clute was a thirty-one-year-old saddler from New York and the original first sergeant of Company A, 5th Texas. He was promoted to first lieutenant on November 7, 1861. From February through April, 1862, he was detailed to recruit for the regiment in Texas. A number of men, Campbell among them, signed up to serve with the unit during Clute's mission. This was the only significant addition of recruits to the 5th Texas during the war. Clute returned to Virginia in time for the campaigns during the spring of 1862. He was killed at Gaines's Mill on June 27, 1862. Simpson, *Hood's Texas Brigade: A Compendium,* p. 174; Moore, "Men of the Bayou City Guards," p. 166.

14. Forts Henry and Donelson, in northern Tennessee, were captured in mid-February, 1862, by a combined army and navy operation led by Brig. Gen. Ulysses S. Grant and Commodore Andrew H. Foote. For the Union, the capture of the forts was one of their first meaningful successes. For the Confederates, the loss opened a significant hole in their western defensive line. Franklin B. Cooling, *Forts Henry and Donelson: The Key to the Confederate Heartland.*

Chapter 2

1. Joseph Eggleston Johnston was a highly respected general in the antebellum army. He shared command of the Confederate forces at First Manassas with Pierre Gustave Toutant Beauregard. By the end of the war, Johnston had commanded major armies in Virginia, the western theater, and the Carolinas. An ongoing feud with the president of the Confederacy, Jefferson Davis, though, tainted Johnston's service. Craig L. Symonds, *Joseph E. Johnston: A Civil War Biography.*

2. The Confederacy usually named its armies after geographical regions they operated in, while the Union armies were usually named after

prominent rivers. Early in the war, the Confederate armies in Virginia were called by various names, including "Army in Virginia," "Army of Virginia," "Army of the Potomac," and "Army of Potomac." By the time Campbell arrived in Virginia, Johnston's army near Washington was being referred to as the "Potomac" army, and Maj. Gen. John Magruder's troops around Yorktown were referred to as the "Virginia" army or "Yorktown" army. Also about this time, Robert E. Lee was brought to Richmond as Jefferson Davis's military advisor, and the troops in the region began to be referred to as the Army of (or in) Northern Virginia. U.S. War Department, comp., *The War of the Rebellion: A Compilation of the Official Records of the Union and Confederate Armies,* ser. 1, vol. 5, pt. 1, pp. 1081 – 82. (Cited hereafter as *OR,* all references to series 1 unless otherwise indicated.) As early as February 25, Johnston was addressed as "Commanding, Army of Northern Virginia," by A. L. Rives, acting chief, Engineer Bureau. *OR,* vol. 5, pt. 1, p. 1090; vol. 11, pt. 3, pp. 397, 408 – 409. Robert E. Lee addressed Johnston as "Commanding, Army of Northern Virginia," on March 5 and March 28, 1862, but addressed him as "Commanding, Army in Northern Virginia," on March 25. After Lee took command of the consolidated forces around Richmond in June, 1862, the army became known for all time as the Army of Northern Virginia.

3. George B. McClellan came out of Ohio to win early, though minor, victories in western Virginia. McClellan excelled at organizing the army into a strong fighting force, but he stumbled and delayed when the time came to take the army into the field. His second turn commanding the Army of the Potomac ended when he failed to follow up the advantage gained at Antietam. His bid for the presidency in 1864 looked like it would be successful until Federal success on the battlefield late in the year swayed public support back to Pres. Abraham Lincoln. McClellan remained active in politics and was New Jersey's governor from the late 1870s into the 1880s. Stephen W. Sears, *George B. McClellan: The Young Napoleon.* Campbell consistently misspells the general's name as "McLelland."

4. More correctly, Campbell and most Civil War infantrymen were issued "rifle muskets." "Muskets" were smoothbore shoulder weapons in common use before the war and fired round lead balls. A standard musket was fifty-seven inches long. "Rifles" were shorter, about forty-nine inches long, and had spiral grooves, or "rifling," cut into the inside of the barrel. The projectile they fired was conical, with the base end being hollow so as to flare against the rifling when fired. The spin imparted on the projectile by the spiral grooves gave it better accuracy and longer distance. Rifles were used by mounted infantry and other troops who depended on maneuverability. "Rifle muskets" had the length of the old muskets but the barrel rifling of the newer rifles. These were standard weapons for infantry during the Civil War. The Enfield rifle muskets were manufactured in England and imported in great numbers by both sides during the war. The name came from the armory that first designed the weapons. Other armories also supplied them. The weap-

ons were similar to the U.S.-made Springfield-model rifle muskets. Earl J. Coates and Dean S. Thomas, *An Introduction to Civil War Small Arms,* pp. 19, 82 – 83.

5. Campbell's numbers seem questionable. A regulation-strength company numbered about 100 men. Muster Roll 7, covering the time period March 1 – April 30, 1862, lists 109 men reporting for duty, including 41 men ill or on detached service. The original company had been supplemented by fifty-one enlistments in March, 1862, but had been reduced by forty-one through promotions, discharges, illnesses, accidents, and desertions. Moore, "Men of the Bayou City Guards," pp. 104 – 17.

6. Soldiers in a company would form themselves into a "mess," typically comprising four men. They would share cookware and cooking duties and would sometimes pool their resources to buy or otherwise acquire food.

7. The returns for Johnston's army on the Peninsula compiled at the end of April, 1862, show a total of 55,633 men of all arms. *OR,* vol. 11, pt. 3, pp. 479 – 84.

8. Skirmishers were deployed in a line across the front (or in this case the rear) of the main body of troops. The men were spread out, usually at five-yard intervals, and provided a screen against the enemy's advance. Forming squares was to arrange the troops in a box-shaped formation, with the officers in the open center. It was designed particularly as a defense against attack by cavalry.

9. Among Confederate forces that bore the brunt of the fighting at the Battle of Williamsburg were the brigades commanded by Brigadier Generals Jubal A. Early, Ambrose Powell Hill, George E. Pickett, Cadmus M. Wilcox, and Raleigh E. Colston and Colonels Micah Jenkins and Roger Pryor. *OR,* vol. 11, pt. 1, pp. 567, 569.

10. John B. Magruder was born in Virginia in 1807. Following graduation from West Point in 1830, his antebellum military experience included distinguished service in the Mexican War and subsequent postings from coast to coast across the United States. Magruder was nicknamed "Prince John" for the appearance and attitude he affected. During the defense of Williamsburg, he stage managed a performance of his command to bluff McClellan into believing that the Confederates were stronger than they were. Magruder's star fell during the Seven Days Battles, when his excited manner led to rumors of drunkenness. He was sent west, where he energetically campaigned in Texas. Following the war, Magruder went to Mexico and served in Maximilian's army. He subsequently returned to the United States, dying in Texas in 1871. Davis, *Confederate General,* vol. 4, pp. 138 – 41.

11. William Henry Chase Whiting was a West Point graduate, class of 1845. Prior to the war, he had served in the engineers. Whiting commanded a division in the Army of Northern Virginia up through the Seven Days Battles and later served in the Department of North Carolina. Whiting was wounded and captured at Fort Fisher. He died of his wounds, a prisoner, on March 10, 1865. Ibid., vol. 6, pp. 132 – 33.

12. Maj. Gen. Gustavus Smith was a senior general in the Virginia theater. When Johnston was wounded at Seven Pines on May 31, 1862, Smith took command of the Army of Potomac. By the next day, Smith had yielded command to Gen. Robert E. Lee. Smith resigned his commission in February, 1863, after several junior generals were promoted over him. Smith later returned to service with the Georgia militia. Leonne M. Hudson, *The Odyssey of a Southerner: The Life and Times of Gustavus Woodson Smith.*

13. William Buel Franklin graduated first in his 1843 West Point class. He served in the prewar army as an engineer, seeing combat in the Mexican War. Franklin commanded a brigade at First Manassas and rose to corps command by the time of the Peninsula campaign. Franklin's work in the failed Federal attack at Fredericksburg in December, 1862, drew sharp criticism from his commander, Maj. Gen. Ambrose Burnside. He was transferred to the Gulf Department and was wounded during the Red River expedition. John T. Hubbell and James W. Geary, ed., *Biographical Dictionary of the Union: Northern Leaders of the Civil War,* pp. 186 – 87.

14. Campbell probably refers to Paul E. McCullough, a twenty-three-year-old barkeeper from New York City, who was also recruited in March, 1862. He was reported missing during the retreat from Yorktown on May 5, 1862, but later rejoined the unit and was wounded and captured at Darbytown Road, October 7, 1864. McCullough was paroled May 14, 1865. Simpson, *Hood's Texas Brigade: A Compendium,* p. 178; Moore, "Men of the Bayou City Guards," p. 166.

15. Evander McIvor Law began the war as a captain, commanding a company of Alabama troops and soon was promoted to lieutenant colonel of the 4th Alabama. Following a severe wound at First Manassas, Law was promoted to colonel of the regiment. His troops fought with distinction at Gettysburg and Chickamauga. Law also fought well in the 1864 spring campaign. He was wounded at Cold Harbor and finished the war fighting in North Carolina. Law eventually attained the rank of major general and command of a division. Davis, *Confederate General,* vol. 4, pp. 22 – 25.

16. The battle was referred to as "West Point," or "Eltham's Landing," and also sometimes "Barhamsville." West Point is on a small peninsula in the Pamunkey River, where it enters into the York River. The fighting took place south of the Pamunkey River, between Eltham and Barhamsville, and directly across the river from West Point. *OR,* vol. 11, pt. 1, p. 627.

17. This was probably Capt. W. D. Denny. He had been appointed commissary sergeant on November 24, 1861. He was promoted to captain and was made regimental commissary officer in January, 1862. Denny was killed at Eltham's Landing on May 7, 1862. Simpson, *Hood's Texas Brigade: A Compendium,* p. 169.

18. Campbell's company had existed before the war as a militia unit, the Bayou City Guards. Moore, "Men of the Bayou City Guards," p. 14.

19. Union casualties at the Battle of West Point, or Eltham's Landing, to-

taled 186. Seven officers and 41 enlisted men were killed, six officers and 104 enlisted men were wounded, and 28 enlisted men were captured or missing. *OR,* vol. 11, pt. 1, p. 618.

20. Franklin's division numbered 11,332. Whiting commanded a division of 6,545 men. Of that, the Texas Brigade numbered 1,922, Hampton's brigade, 2,225, and Whiting's old brigade 2,398. Ibid., pt. 3, pp. 230, 483.

21. The Texas Brigade suffered losses of eight killed and twenty-eight wounded. *OR,* vol. 11, pt. 1, p. 627.

22. Wade Hampton was born in Charleston, South Carolina. In addition to having reportedly the largest land holdings in the South, he was a South Carolina legislator before the war. Hampton organized the Hampton Legion, paying for its equipment himself. He proved to be an extremely capable commander, first of infantry and later of cavalry. After the war, Hampton returned to political life, serving as governor of South Carolina and as a U.S. senator. Davis, *Confederate General,* vol. 3, pp. 50 – 53.

    A "legion" was a unit of combined arms approximately the size of a regiment. The Hampton Legion (or Hampton's South Carolina Legion) initially comprised seven infantry companies, four cavalry companies, and an artillery company. Prior to Eltham's Landing, the legion had been broken up. The infantry was included in a brigade under Hampton's command. Hampton's brigade was broken up after the general was wounded at Seven Pines. The infantry of Hampton's Legion was then assigned to the Texas Brigade. In November, 1862, the brigades of the Army of Northern Virginia were reorganized by state, and the legion's infantry was reassigned to a South Carolina brigade under Brig. Gen. Micah Jenkins. Simpson, *Hood's Texas Brigade: A Compendium,* pp. 107 – 108, 194.

23. Nicholas A. Davis was the 4th Texas Infantry's original chaplain. He was detached from the regiment for recruiting service in Texas from February through April, 1862, and then absent on duty in Richmond the latter part of 1862 through mid-1863. In November, 1863, Davis resigned from the army. Simpson, *Hood's Texas Brigade: A Compendium,* p. 92. Nicholas A. Davis, *The Campaign from Texas to Maryland with the Battle of Fredericksburg.* Chaplain Davis's description of the first two years of the war was originally published in Richmond. A second edition, with some omissions and corrections, was published later the same year in Houston. An expanded edition, edited by Donald Everett, was published under the title, *Chaplain Davis and Hood's Texas Brigade,* in 1962.

24. William Barksdale was born in Tennessee, studied law in Mississippi, and then worked as a newspaper editor in Columbus. He enlisted in the army during the Mexican War and attained an officer's rank. Barksdale then turned to politics, representing Mississippi in Congress up to the state's secession. Barksdale fought well throughout the early campaigns of the war, working his way to the rank of brigadier general. He was mortally wounded at Gettysburg on July 2, 1863, dying in enemy hands the next day. Davis, *Confederate General,* vol. 1, pp.58 – 59.

25. "Bayou City Guards' Song in the Chickahominy Swamp" told the tale of Campbell's company in action in the vicinity of the Chickahominy. Francis D. Allan, comp., *Allan's Lone Star Ballads: A Collection of Southern Patriotic Songs Made during Confederate Times*, pp. 153 – 54.

26. The exact passage reads, "Here we found several Generals, with their attendant aides and couriers, all exhorting us to 'close up,' and for God's sake to hurry." Davis differs on the time also, giving it as "1 o'clock at night." He goes on to describe General Whiting's frustrations at trying to get his men through the mud and across the stream. Davis, *Campaign from Texas to Maryland*, p. 37.

27. A Virginia artillerist described the concoctions that the soldiers knew so well. Commenting on the sparse ingredients available for meals, he wrote: "The result is that 'slosh' or 'coosh' must do. So the bacon is fried out till the pan is half full of boiling grease. The flour is mixed with water until it flows like milk, poured into the grease and rapidly stirred till the whole is a dirty brown mixture. It is now ready to be served. Perhaps some dainty fellow prefers the more imposing 'slapjack.' If so, the flour is mixed with less water, the grease reduced, and the paste poured in till it covers the bottom of the pan, and, when brown on the underside, is, by a nimble twist of the pan, turned and browned again. If there is any sugar in camp it makes a delicious addition." Carlton McCarthy, *Detailed Minutiae of Soldier Life in the Army of Northern Virginia*, 1861–1865, p. 59.

28. As winter ended in 1862, Joseph E. Johnston positioned his Confederate army between Washington, D.C., and Richmond. The Federal army was in Washington, and Johnston wanted to be able to meet it along whichever route to Richmond it chose to take. Union commander George McClellan chose a water route, taking his army by ship to the tip of the Peninsula, between the York and James Rivers. There an outmanned Confederate force dug a series of defensive positions at Yorktown, Williamsburg, and outside of Richmond. Once the direction of the Federal attack became clear to Johnston, he moved troops to the Peninsula and took command there. Determining that the forward positions were weak, Johnston ordered the retreat of the Rebel troops from Yorktown to Williamsburg. McClellan, in the meantime, had been at work building his troop strength. When he finally attacked at Yorktown, the rebels were gone. McClellan followed Johnston up the Peninsula to a battle with the Confederate rear guard at Williamsburg. The Confederates maintained an orderly retreat back to the Richmond defenses.

Once outside of Richmond, the Chickahominy River divided McClellan's army into two parts. Johnston determined to attack the two corps south of the rain-swollen river, hoping to defeat them before the three corps north of the river could cross. The resulting Confederate attack at Seven Pines on May 31, 1862, was poorly executed. Federal positions were overrun, but the Confederates could not deliver a finishing blow. Union troops from north of the Chickahominy came on to the field late in the day, checking the Rebel attack. The next day saw little decisive action, and the battle ended with the armies about where they had started.

The fighting at Seven Pines had a major effect on the war, though. Late on the first day, Johnston was severely wounded while examining the positions of the troops. Command evolved to Maj. Gen. Gustavus Smith, but only for one day. Smith was in ill health, and command of the Confederate troops was then given to Gen. Robert E. Lee. Lee strengthened his defensive lines around Richmond and then began a bold offensive to drive McClellan from the Peninsula. He divided his army, leaving one part to defend the capital against a much larger force and marching another part north of the Chickahominy. He planned to join forces with Maj. Gen. Thomas "Stonewall" Jackson's army coming out of the Shenandoah Valley and then to strike at the Union troops guarding McClellan's supply line. The Confederate attack was poorly coordinated, and Brig. Gen. Fitz John Porter's Federals were able to hold their position. McClellan, however, decided to change his base of operations and fought a series of engagements as he worked his way to a new supply base along the James River on the southern shore of the Peninsula. Collectively known as the Seven Days Battles, the action was marked by fierce fighting and poorly coordinated Confederate attacks. The final result was the Union army moved away from Richmond but remained in the area with a base of operations on the Peninsula. Joseph P. Cullen, *The Peninsula Campaign, 1862;* Gary W. Gallagher, ed., *The Richmond Campaign of 1862: The Peninsula and the Seven Days;* Stephen W. Sears, *To the Gates of Richmond: The Peninsula Campaign.*

29. Union forces (112,392) outnumbered their Confederate counterparts (55,633) two to one. About 400 Union soldiers were captured at the battles of Williamsburg and West Point. In his own after-action report, however, General Johnston admitted having to leave 400 wounded Confederate soldiers "who were not in condition to be moved" in Williamsburg and having to abandon five field pieces at the Williamsburg wharf "for want of horses and harnesses." *OR*, vol. 11, pt. 3, pp. 130, 484; pt. 1, pp. 276, 450, 618.

Chapter 3

1. Campbell here refers to Alexis Theodore Rainey, the original captain of Company H. Rainey was born in Alabama in 1822 and moved to Texas in 1854, where he became a lawyer and legislator. Enlisting early in the war, Rainey was promoted to major on October 1, 1861, to lieutenant colonel on October 21, and to colonel on January 3, 1862. Rainey was wounded at Gaines's Mill on June 27, 1862. He was assigned to duty in Texas on September 4, 1863, and in July, 1864, was dropped from the rolls. Rainey died in Texas in 1891. Krick, *Lee's Colonels,* pp. 312 – 13.
2. Phillip A. Work was the original captain of Company F, 1st Texas. His promotion to lieutenant colonel was dated May 19, 1862. Work's career was marked by illness, culminating in his resignation on January 5, 1864. Simpson, *Hood's Texas Brigade: A Compendium,* p. 10.

3. Matt Dale was born in Nashville, Tennessee, and moved to Texas in 1852. He began the war as a lieutenant of Company G, 1st Texas. He was promoted to major on May 19, 1862. Dale was killed at Sharpsburg on September 17, 1862. Krick, *Lee's Colonels,* p. 109.

4. D. C. Farmer was a twenty-five-year-old teacher from Kentucky and the original third lieutenant of Company A. He was promoted to captain on November 1, 1861, made acting major of the regiment on October 31, 1863, and then acting lieutenant colonel two months later. Farmer was wounded at Gettysburg and the Wilderness. In the summer of 1864 he was sent back to Texas on recruiting duty. Simpson, *Hood's Texas Brigade: A Compendium,* p. 173; Moore, "Men of the Bayou City Guards," p. 161.

5. John Hale was the original second lieutenant of Company A. He was promoted to first lieutenant on November 7, 1861. Hale's service with the regiment ended in December, 1862, when he was transferred to the pioneer corps. Simpson, *Hood's Texas Brigade: A Compendium,* p. 173.

6. B. P. (Belcher Pulaski) Fuller was born in Beaufort, North Carolina, on April 13, 1836. He was an attorney before the war but enlisted as a private. Fuller was promoted straight to third lieutenant, then to second lieutenant after Gaines's Mill, and to first lieutenant on September 1, 1863. He was wounded at the Wilderness on May 6, 1864, and was ill in Richmond that fall. Ibid., p. 174; Moore, "Men of the Bayou City Guards," p. 162.

7. Thomas W. Fitzgerald was a twenty-one-year-old printer at the time of his enlistment in March, 1862. His bravery earned him the position of regimental color sergeant in July, 1862. He was wounded and captured at Gettysburg, paroled, and then wounded again at Cold Harbor. Fitzgerald finished the war in Texas in the invalid corps. Simpson, *Hood's Texas Brigade: A Compendium,* p. 170; Moore, "Men of the Bayou City Guards," p. 161.

8. Owen O'Malley was a twenty-eight-year-old civil engineer when he enlisted on July 19, 1861. He was wounded and captured at Second Manassas. Following parole, he rejoined the unit and was wounded at Chickamauga. Granted a furlough to Texas, O'Malley did not return and was recorded as AWOL. Simpson, *Hood's Texas Brigade: A Compendium,* p. 179; Moore, "Men of the Bayou City Guards," p. 169.

9. Company records do not report a W. P. Morell. Campbell might be referring to William B. Ferrell, who was detailed to the Texas Brigade Hospital in Richmond on September 19, 1862. Captured at Spotsylvania on May 10, 1864, Ferrell was exchanged on January 17, 1865. Simpson, *Hood's Texas Brigade: A Compendium,* p. 176.

10. Union brigadier general Silas Casey commanded the 3d Division in Brig. Gen. Erasmus Keyes's IV Corps. On May 20, 1862, Casey dispatched a combined force of infantry and artillery from his division on a reconnaissance along the Williamsburg Stage Road toward Richmond. McClellan had ordered his forces split on either side of the Chickahominy River, and Casey's division led the advance as they forded the river near Bottom's Bridge. The balance of the IV Corps

crossed south of the Chickahominy soon afterward, followed by the Union III Corps under Brig. Gen. Samuel Heintzelman. McClellan placed Heintzelman in overall command of the two corps south of the river. *OR,* vol. 11, pt. 1, pp. 640 – 49; Sears, *To the Gates of Richmond,* pp. 109 – 10, 113, 124.

11. Silas Casey was a thirty-five-year veteran of the Regular Army when the war broke out. He had been brevetted twice during the Mexican War for his brave conduct while serving with Maj. Gen. Winfield Scott. Casey was appointed brigadier general of volunteers on August 31, 1861. His troops were heavily engaged at Seven Pines, being attacked in the positions Campbell describes here. Casey spent much of the remainder of the war in the Washington D.C. area. His influence reached well beyond that city, though, as his book of infantry tactics was a standard instruction manual for the U.S. Army during the war. Hubbell and Geary, *Biographical Dictionary,* pp. 88 – 89.

12. James Longstreet was a class of 1842 West Point graduate who had served in the U.S. Army and the Mexican War. Longstreet led troops in most of the major battles in the Virginia theater, beginning with First Manassas. He also led an independent command to Chickamauga, where he cooperated successfully with Gen. Braxton Bragg, and to Knoxville, where his siege of the city was much less successful. After the war, Longstreet came to terms with the U.S. government, serving as minister to Turkey and later as commissioner of Pacific Railroads under two presidents. The general died in 1904, the last survivor of the Confederate high command. Jeffry D. Wert, *General James Longstreet: The Confederacy's Most Controversial Soldier, a Biography.*

13. On the evening of May 30, 1862, Longstreet's division and the divisions of Major Generals D. H. Hill, Benjamin Huger, and Gustavus W. Smith, all under Longstreet's direction, were in positions astride the Williamsburg Road and Nine Mile Road on the eastern outskirts of Richmond. These units were poised to strike the Union lines south of the Chickahominy River early the next day. *OR,* vol. 11, pt. 1, pp. 933 – 35, 939 – 41; Sears, *To the Gates of Richmond,* pp. 117 – 20.

14. The 2d Florida Infantry, commanded by Col. E. A. Perry, was the only regiment from that state engaged at the Battle of Seven Pines. A part of Brig. Gen. Samuel Garland's brigade of Maj. Gen. D. H. Hill's division, the 2d Florida distinguished itself in action along the Williamsburg Road. *Battles and Leaders of the Civil War,* vol. 2, p. 219; J. J. Dickison, *Military History of Florida,* pp. 146 – 47.

15. Robert Hopkins Hatton was Ohio born and Tennessee educated, a lawyer and politician prior to the war. As a colonel commanding the 7th Tennessee Infantry, he fought in western Virginia, and on May 23, 1862, he was promoted to brigadier general. On May 31 of that year, Hatton was killed leading his troops in an attack at Fair Oaks Station. Davis, *Confederate General,* vol. 3, pp. 72 – 73.

16. James Johnston Pettigrew was born in North Carolina on July 4, 1828. He was a student at the University of North Carolina by age fifteen and appointed assistant professor at the Naval Observatory in Washington

upon his graduation at age nineteen. Pettigrew later turned to law and politics, and as a colonel of militia he was in Charleston Harbor for the bombing of Fort Sumter. By February, 1862, Pettigrew had been commissioned a brigadier general. He was badly wounded and captured at Seven Pines, exchanged two months later. Following a period in charge of defensive positions, he was returned to the field. Pettigrew gained command of a division at Gettysburg after his superior was wounded. There he was in the thick of the third day's fighting. During the retreat after the battle, Pettigrew was wounded in a rear-guard action and died three days later. Ibid., vol. 5, pp.24 – 25.

17. Confederate brigadier general W. H. C. Whiting's division, which included the 5th Texas Infantry, assailed the Federal divisions of Brigadier Generals John Sedgwick and Darius Couch on May 31, 1862. These two Union divisions included the 7th, 10th, 15th, 19th, and 20th Massachusetts Infantry Regiments. After the Confederate attacks ceased at nightfall, some Federal units mounted spontaneous counterattacks. Sears, *To the Gates of Richmond*, pp. 137 – 39, 369 – 71.

18. Campbell refers to the Richmond and York River Railroad in the vicinity of Fair Oaks Station. Ibid., p. 139.

19. Hood's brigade lost thirteen wounded. *OR*, vol. 11, pt. 2, p. 506.

20. The Confederates lost over 6,000 men: 980 killed, 4,749 wounded, and 405 captured or missing. *Battles and Leaders*, vol. 2, p. 219.

21. Federal losses totaled 5,031 men: 790 killed, 3,594 wounded, and 647 captured or missing. Before retiring to their original lines, Confederate troops scoured the abandoned Union campsites for any useful supplies. *OR*, vol. 11, pt. 1, pp. 757 – 62; Sears, *To the Gates of Richmond*, p. 148.

22. Robert Edward Lee continued a family military tradition, graduating second in his West Point class and serving with distinction, first as an engineer and then in the Mexican War. Lee led his Army of Northern Virginia into everlasting fame, it being recognized as one of the world's great armies despite two less-than-successful advances into the North. Lee built his reputation upon strong defensive works and daring offensive maneuvers. He also developed a reputation for caring for his troops that prompted in them an extreme devotion to their general. After the war Lee returned to civilian life as president of struggling Washington College (now Washington and Lee University). There he quietly led the South by example back into the Union until his death on October 12, 1870. Emory M. Thomas, *Robert E. Lee;* Douglas Southall Freeman, *R. E. Lee: A Biography.*

Chapter 4

1. Combined Confederate forces in and around Richmond under Lee's command came to about 92,400. Sears, *To the Gates of Richmond*, pp. 195, 416 n. 11.

2. Maj. Gen. D. H. Hill's division, located in proximity to the Texas Brigade, included the 5th, 6th, 12th, 13th, and 26th Alabama Infantry Regiments. Ibid., pp. 139 (map), 376.

3. Thomas Jonathan Jackson was a Virginian and a graduate of the West Point class of 1846. Jackson's use of troops in the Shenandoah Valley became legendary. He came out of the valley to join Robert E. Lee for the Seven Days Battles and the campaigns that followed. On May 2, 1863, after a successful assault on the Federal right at Chancellorsville, Jackson was badly wounded by his own men during an evening reconnaissance. He developed pneumonia and died on May 10, 1863. James I. Robertson Jr., *Stonewall Jackson: The Man, the Soldier, the Legend.*

4. John Cunningham Upton was born in Tennessee in 1823. He went looking for gold in California in 1850. Nine years later he moved to Texas. Upton was captain of Company B during the first months of the war. When Walter B. Botts resigned, Upton was promoted to lieutenant colonel. He was killed at the Battle of Second Manassas, August 30, 1862. Krick, *Lee's Colonels,* p. 378.

5. Richard Stoddert Ewell was an 1840 West Point graduate who served in the Southwest before the war. He was commissioned a brigadier general on June 17, 1861, and rose to take over Stonewall Jackson's corps following the latter's death. Ewell lost a leg during the Second Manassas campaign but remained in the field until ill health forced him from active duty in 1864. Given command of Richmond's defenses, he was captured at Sayler's Creek on April 6, 1865. Ewell had proven to be a capable commander until given corps command, at which point he seemed overmatched. Davis, *Confederate General,* vol. 2, pp. 110 – 13.

6. Nathaniel Prentiss Banks was a Massachusetts-born political general. Defeated by Stonewall Jackson in the Shenandoah Valley and at Cedar Mountain during 1862, Banks then went west, where he led the ill-fated Red River Campaign. Once out of the army, he was elected to the U.S. Congress, where his conduct seemed to be guided by personal and political enrichment. Hubbell and Geary, *Biographical Dictionary,* p. 25.

7. Robert Huston Milroy was born in Indiana in 1816. He went to Vermont to study at Norwich University. After two years service in the Mexican War, he turned to the study of law and was a practicing attorney in Indiana when the Civil War started. Milroy began the war as the colonel of the 9th Indiana Infantry, campaigning under McClellan in western Virginia. He gained promotion, ultimately reaching major general. From western Virginia, Milroy went to the Shenandoah, where he fought against Stonewall Jackson. Milroy's time as a field commander came to an end in June, 1863, when his command was severely beaten at Second Winchester. The general escaped capture but was later subjected to a court of inquiry, which ultimately exonerated him. After the war he became a canal company trustee and later an Indian agent. Robert Milroy died in Olympia, Washington, in 1890. Ibid., p. 357.

8. James Shields was born in Ireland in 1810. He came to the United States as a teenager, already classically educated. Practicing law and politics in Illinois prior to the Mexican War, he served as a brigadier general of Illinois troops during that conflict. When the Civil War broke out, Shields was commissioned a brigadier general of volunteers. His defeat

at the hands of Stonewall Jackson in the Shenandoah Valley was followed by his resignation in 1863. Shields moved to Missouri, filling an unexpired Senate term from that state. He died while on a lecture tour on June 1, 1879. Ezra J. Warner, *Generals in Blue,* pp. 444–45.

9. John Charles Frémont was born in Savannah, Georgia, in 1813. He was appointed to the army topographical engineers and, in the years leading up to the Mexican War, led several significant expeditions in the West. As the presidential candidate of the newly formed Republican Party, Frémont lost the 1856 election to James Buchanan. After the Civil War began, Lincoln appointed him as a major general in the Regular Army. In a succession of commands Frémont proved to be both a political and a military liability. Following assignment to Pope's command in 1862, Frémont requested, and was granted, his release. He was nominated for president in 1864 by a coalition of Radical Republicans and War Democrats. Lincoln's supporters struck a deal with him to pull out in return for the ouster of conservative Montgomery Blair from the cabinet. Frémont died in New York City in 1890. Hubbell and Geary, *Biographical Dictionary,* p. 187.

10. For three months beginning in March, 1862, Confederate major general Thomas J. "Stonewall" Jackson executed a succession of skillful and daring maneuvers in the Shenandoah Valley against three separate Union armies whose combined strength outnumbered his own two to one. Jackson's troops were victorious in sharp engagements against Union forces under Maj. Gen. John C. Frémont at McDowell, May 8, 1862; Maj. Gen. Nathaniel Banks at Front Royal, May 23, and again at the First Battle of Winchester, May 25; Frémont again at Cross Keys, June 8; and finally Brig. Gen. James Shields at Port Republic, June 9. *OR,* vol. 12, pt. 1, pp. 379–80, 701–16; *Battles and Leaders,* vol. 2, pp. 282–301.

11. The three railroads Campbell alludes to were the Virginia Central; the Richmond, Fredericksburg, and Potomac; and the Richmond and York River. U.S. War Department, comp., *Atlas to Accompany the Official Records of the Union and Confederate Armies* (reprinted as *The Official Military Atlas of the Civil War*), plate 20, map 1.

12. Each day about two hundred Texans from the brigade acted as scouts, spies, and sharpshooters, often well beyond the regular picket lines. Mrs. A. V. Winkler, *The Confederate Capital and Hood's Texas Brigade,* pp. 22, 23.

13. Campbell incorrectly identifies the Alabama brigade's commander, who was actually Col. Evander Law. *OR,* vol. 11, pt. 2, pp. 552.

14. Alexander Robert Lawton was born in South Carolina in 1818. He studied military science at West Point and then law at Harvard. Following graduation from Harvard Law School, Lawton settled in Savannah, Georgia, to practice law. There he also became president of the Augusta and Savannah Railroad and served in the Georgia legislature. At the outbreak of hostilities, Lawton was appointed a brigadier general. He fought well in the Seven Days Campaign. At Sharpsburg Lawton was badly wounded. Following that, he was placed in command of the

Quartermaster General's Department, a position he served in for the remainder of the war. After the surrender, Lawton returned to the practice of law and politics and in 1887 was appointed minister to Austria. Lawton died in 1896. Davis, *Confederate General*, vol. 4, pp. 26 – 29.

15. The addition of Whiting's division increased Jackson's strength to 18,500. Robertson, *Stonewall Jackson*, pp. 455 – 58.

16. D. (Dempsy) W. Walker was a thirty-seven-year-old printer from Mississippi. One of the original members of the company, Walker died of a wound suffered at Second Manassas, August 30, 1862. Simpson, *Hood's Texas Brigade: A Compendium*, p. 181; Moore, "Men of the Bayou City Guards," p. 176.

Chapter 5

1. The rumors proved unfounded – no other Texas units would join the brigade during the war.

2. A brigade of infantry from South Carolina and four brigades from North Carolina reinforced the Army of Northern Virginia following the Battle of Seven Pines. Including Jackson's 18,500 men, Lee confronted McClellan with 92,400 soldiers. Sears, *To the Gates of Richmond*, p. 156.

3. Ambrose Powell Hill was a native Virginian and an 1847 West Point graduate. He fought in Mexico and subsequently served in Texas and Florida. Hill attained the rank of major general in the Confederate army by the end of the Peninsula Campaign. He fought aggressively throughout the 1862 campaigns in Virginia and Maryland. When Lee reorganized the army after Stonewall Jackson's death, Hill was given command of the newly created III Corps. He struggled as a corps commander. Hill's war and life ended on April 2, 1865, when he was killed trying to reach his troops on the Petersburg line. Davis, *Confederate General*, vol. 3, pp. 96 – 99.

4. James Ewell Brown Stuart, Lee's cavalry commander, was born in Virginia in 1833. He graduated from West Point in 1854 and served on the frontier. During the Civil War, Stuart quickly built a reputation for daring and flamboyance. The "ride" Campbell refers to began with Lee's directive to Stuart to scout McClellan's right flank. But he did that and more, riding around McClellan's entire army. Stuart continued to serve as Lee's cavalry commander until he was fatally wounded fighting Federal cavalry at Yellow Tavern in May, 1864. Emory M. Thomas, *Bold Dragoon: The Life of J. E. B. Stuart*.

5. Campbell refers to Cold Harbor.

6. Forty rounds filled a cartridge box, but it was not uncommon for the men to be issued extra rounds before going into battle. The balance remaining after filling the box would be crammed into the soldiers' pockets or haversacks.

7. John W. Stevens, another 5th Texas veteran, also recounts the story of the bugler "Sandy" and his prisoners. He explains the bugler's accent as being due to his German heritage. Stevens reports the prisoner count to be

twenty-two. John W. Stevens, *Reminiscences of the Civil War,* pp. 25 – 26.

8. Confederate major general Ambrose Powell Hill's division, nearest Gaines's Mill, was comprised of troops from several states, including North and South Carolina and Virginia. They opened the battle at midafternoon on June 27, 1862. Brig. Gen. Charles W. Field's brigade in Hill's division included four infantry regiments from Virginia, which made several gallant attacks against what Field described afterward as "an infantry fire that nothing could live under." *OR,* vol. 11, pt. 2, pp. 487 – 88, 834 – 37, 841 – 43.

9. According to regulations, by the summer of 1862, the regiments in the Army of Northern Virginia were supposed to carry only the army's recognized battle flag – the square red flag with a blue St. Andrew's Cross and white stars and trim. But the Texas regiments, and some others, continued to carry state flags well into the war. Nicholas Davis describes watching a review of the troops on October 8, 1862, by Generals Longstreet and Hood. As the men passed, particular notice was taken of the 5th Texas' flag, a "Lone Star" banner pierced by bullet and shell fragments forty-seven times, having had seven men go down carrying it. Next in formation was the 4th Texas, whose flag was even more battle scarred and had been carried by nine bearers who had been wounded or killed. The parade marked the last appearance of that 4th Texas flag. It was retired and sent home as a treasure too valuable to remain in the field. Ibid., vol. 5, p. 969; vol. 51, pt. 2, p. 632; Sumrall, *Battle Flags;* Davis, *Campaign from Texas to Maryland,* pp. 97 – 99.

10. George Onderdonk was an original private of the company. He was made regimental color sergeant on November 25, 1861, later promoted to fifth sergeant and then to second sergeant. At Gaines's Mill he was wounded in the arm. After being furloughed to Texas, Onderdonk was discharged for disability on April 6, 1863. He took up the carriage-making trade in Houston. Campbell had pasted into the ledger book a newspaper clipping of a tribute to Onderdonk. He wrote a note explaining: "The above gentleman was a friend, and member of my company when shot down at 'Gaines Mill.' He leaned upon his elbow, held the flag aloft until it was taken from him by an uninjured comrade. 'Requiscat in pace' (RC)." Simpson, *Hood's Texas Brigade: A Compendium,* p. 170; Moore, "Men of the Bayou City Guards," p. 30.

11. Campbell probably refers here to Sam H. Watson, an original member of Company E. He was wounded at Gaines's Mill and again at Gettysburg, where he was also captured. Amputating his wounded arm failed to save his life, and Watson died on September 13, 1863. Simpson, *Hood's Texas Brigade: A Compendium,* p. 210.

12. W. P. McGowan was the original second sergeant of the company. He was promoted several times, eventually becoming regimental adjutant on February 19, 1864. He was wounded at the Wilderness on May 6, 1864, and was paroled at Appomattox on April 12, 1865. Ibid., p. 168.

13. While engaged in a bitter, nearly three-hour firefight against troops from Whiting's division, the 4th New Jersey Infantry, Col. James H. Simpson commanding, was surrounded by "overwhelming" enemy

forces and surrendered to Hood's Texans. The hapless Union regiment listed 437 officers and enlisted men captured or missing after what had been their "first time under immediate fire." *OR*, vol. 11, pt. 2, pp. 34, 40, 444 – 46.

14. The largest and bloodiest fight of the Peninsula Campaign, the Battle of Gaines's Mill cost the victorious Confederates 1,483 killed, 6,402 wounded, and 108 captured or missing. Sears, *To the Gates of Richmond*, p. 249.

15. William A. George was a seventeen-year-old laborer from Nassau and an original private in Company A. He was detailed to the pioneer corps in December, 1862, and was surrendered with the army at Appomattox in 1865. Following the war, George went into business in Houston with another early recruit, J. Davidson, forming the George and Davidson Company. Simpson, *Hood's Texas Brigade: A Compendium*, p. 177; Moore, "Men of the Bayou City Guards," pp. 84, 162.

16. The Federal dead numbered 894, compared to the 1,483 Confederates. *OR*, vol. 11, pt. 2., pp. 39 – 41; Sears, *To the Gates of Richmond*, p. 249.

17. W. J. Riley was recruited about the same time as Campbell, March 29, 1862, in Houston. He was thirty-two at the time. Riley was wounded at Second Manassas on August 30, 1862. He died of pneumonia in Winchester, Virginia, on October 18, 1862. Simpson, *Hood's Texas Brigade: A Compendium*, p. 179; Moore, "Men of the Bayou City Guards," p. 171.

18. The loss of the Texas brigade amounted to 86 killed, 481 wounded, and 4 missing from a total of 1,922 men. *OR*, vol. 11, pt. 2, p. 973; pt. 3, p. 483.

19. Magruder's Division comprised the brigades of Generals Howell Cobb and Richard Griffith (commanded at Malvern Hill by Colonel William Barksdale due to the mortal wounding of Griffith two days previous to the episode described here), plus Colonel Stephen D. Lee's artillery. Magruder had a larger overall command consisting of his own division and the divisions of Generals David R. Jones and Lafayette McLaws. In this battle he also employed the divisions of Generals Benjamin Huger and Theophilus H. Holmes. *OR*, vol. 11, pt. 2, pp. 485 – 88; Sears, *To the Gates of Richmond*, pp. 312 – 36, 389 – 91.

20. Ike N. M. Turner was the original captain of Company K, 5th Texas. At twenty-two years of age, he was also the youngest company commander in the brigade. Turner was acting major during the winter of 1862 – 63. While the brigade was detached with Longstreet to the Suffolk, Virginia, area in the spring of 1863, Turner was given command of a battalion of sharpshooters. He was killed at Suffolk on April 14, 1863. Turner's body was sent back to Texas, but its journey was interrupted in Georgia, not to be completed until 1995. Simpson, *Hood's Texas Brigade: A Compendium*, p. 243.

21. Hood's brigade sustained six killed, forty-five wounded, and one missing during the Battle of Malvern Hill. *OR*, vol. 11, pt. 2, p. 567.

22. Benjamin Huger was Charleston born and West Point educated, graduating in 1825. He commanded a number of U.S. arsenals and was chief of ordnance under Winfield Scott in Mexico. He left the U.S. Army

after the fall of Fort Sumter, accepting a position as a brigadier general in the Confederate Army. Huger made major general by October, 1861. He commanded the department that included Norfolk, and when threatened, Huger dismantled the fortifications there and ordered the Confederacy's first ironclad, the CSS *Virginia* (formerly USS *Merrimac*) scuttled. Huger then took command of an infantry division on the Peninsula. His actions during the Seven Days Battles led to censure, a congressional investigation, and his relief as a field commander. Huger was then detailed to inspect artillery and ordnance, and he performed that role capably through the close of the war. Davis, *Confederate General*, vol. 3, pp. 128–29.

23. McClellan, having convinced himself that he was vastly outnumbered by the Confederates, proclaimed in an address to his troops dated July 4, 1862, that the action on the Peninsula, rather than being a failure to take Richmond, had been a brilliant maneuver under extreme pressure to change his base of operations from White House Landing on the Pamunkey River (upstream from the York on the northern edge of the Peninsula) to Harrison's Landing on the James River (on the southern edge of the Peninsula). Throughout the South, McClellan's interpretation of events became the object of ridicule. Sears, *To the Gates of Richmond*, pp. 344–30.

24. Conduct concerning prisoners of war was guided at this time by personal honor, and prisoners were honor-bound to remain prisoners until paroled and to remain out of action until properly exchanged. Jerome B. Robertson, commanding the 5th Texas at Second Manassas, reported a similar situation, writing: "quite a number of prisoners were sent to the rear. I did not weaken my force by sending details with them, but ordered them to the rear unattended by a guard." *OR*, vol. 12, pt. 2, p. 619.

25. Following McClellan's early success in western Virginia, newspapers in the North began referring to him as "The Young Napoleon." It began with the *New York Herald*, but others also took up the phrase. Sears, *McClellan*, pp. 93, 101.

Chapter 6

1. Stephen H. Watkins was one of the recruits gathered in Houston on March 28, 1862. He was wounded at Gettysburg on July 2, 1863. On April 3, 1865, he was captured in Richmond and was paroled on June 22. There were at least a couple of enlisted men in the company who were older than the thirty-seven-year-old Watkins, but most of those soldiers left the service early due to ill health or other physical problems. Watkins may have been the oldest to give long-term service in the field. Simpson, *Hood's Texas Brigade: A Compendium*, p. 181; Moore, "Men of the Bayou City Guards," pp. 153–77.

2. John J. Roberts began the war as a private in Company E, 5th Texas Infantry. On November 15, 1861, he was appointed assistant regimental surgeon. He was wounded on May 6, 1864, at the Wilderness. On Au-

gust 10, Roberts was made regimental surgeon. He was paroled during the surrender at Appomattox. Simpson, *Hood's Texas Brigade: A Compendium*, p. 169.

3. David M. Whaley was a northerner, born in Pennsylvania. He moved to Texas in 1853, becoming a druggist and later serving in the state legislature. The original captain of Company C, on August 22, 1862, Whaley was killed at Freeman's Ford. Krick, *Lee's Colonels*, p. 391.

4. F. M. Poland was a twenty-eight-year-old attorney from Louisiana and an original private in the company. He was detailed as a hospital steward at Marietta, Georgia, on October 19, 1863. On September 17, 1864, Poland was transferred to the Trans-Mississippi Medical Department. After the war he returned to the practice of law. Simpson, *Hood's Texas Brigade: A Compendium*, p. 179; Moore, "Men of the Bayou City Guards," p. 88, 170.

5. Campbell may be mistaken on the name here. Simpson's *Compendium* lists no man named "Cortin" as an officer of any Company C in the brigade. William P. Townsend was the original captain of Company C, 4th Texas, and he was promoted to major on July 10, 1862, during the period Campbell is writing about. Townsend was wounded at Second Manassas on August 30, 1862. He lost a foot as a result and was appointed to a court-martial board in Lt. Gen. William J. Hardee's corps in the Army of Tennessee. Townsend returned to Texas in 1863. Simpson, *Hood's Texas Brigade: A Compendium*, p. 91; Krick, *Lee's Colonels*, p. 374.

6. The Ballard House was one of the most popular gathering places for the rich and powerful in the Confederate capital. Built in the 1850s by John P. Ballard, it was connected by a bridge over the street to another of Ballard's buildings, the Exchange Hotel. The two five-story buildings were among Richmond's tallest, and during times when the fighting drew close to the city, citizens would go to the upper portions of these and other tall buildings to get a view of the proceedings. Judith Brockenbrough McGuire diary quoted in Katharine M. Jones, *Ladies of Richmond: Confederate Capital*, p. 124; Mary Newton Stanard, *Richmond: Its People and Its Story*, pp. 156, 190.

7. C. P. Harn was an original member of the company. He was assigned duty as a scout in November, 1861, and was reported AWOL on May 23, 1862. Harn was dropped from the rolls by special order of General Lee in August, 1863. Simpson, *Hood's Texas Brigade: A Compendium*, p. 177.

8. S. B. Webber was an original private in Company A. He was assigned to duty as a pioneer in November, 1861. He was reported AWOL in July, 1862, and did not return to the unit. Ibid., p. 181.

Chapter 7

1. After taking command of the Federal forces in northern Virginia, Maj. Gen. John Pope issued a letter of introduction in which he stated, "I have come from the West, where we have always seen the backs of our enemies." He went on to contrast his style with that of those who had

preceded him – mainly McClellan's. Subsequent events would make Pope and his letter an inviting target of sarcasm from all sides. *OR,* vol. 12, pt. 3, pp. 473 – 74; John J. Hennessy, *Return to Bull Run: The Campaign and Battle of Second Manassas,* p. 12.

2. Irvin McDowell was born in Columbus, Ohio, on October 15, 1818. He went to school in France before attending West Point, where he graduated in 1839. McDowell later taught at the military academy. In Mexico, he served as aide-de-camp to Brig. Gen. J. E. Wool. In May, 1861, McDowell was commissioned a brigadier general in the Regular Army. This appointment came about through the efforts of Treasury Secretary Salmon Chase – McDowell had never commanded troops. Under political pressure to advance quickly on the new Confederate army, McDowell took his equally green troops south in July, 1861, and was smashed at the First Battle of Manassas. After McClellan took over command of the Federal army in Virginia, McDowell was given a corps and assigned to the defense of the capital. McDowell again led troops in the field at Manassas in August, 1862, and again was badly beaten by the Rebels. He saw little action after that. McDowell remained in the army and retired in 1882, having reached the position of commander, Division of the Pacific. Hubbell and Geary, *Biographical Dictionary,* p. 330.

3. On August 9, 1862, Jackson clashed with Pope's II Corps under Maj. Gen. Nathaniel P. Banks about eight miles south of Culpeper, Virginia. The resulting Battle of Cedar Mountain was less than a brilliant victory for Jackson, whose 24,000 men nearly succumbed to Banks' 9,000 until a strong Confederate counterattack drove the Federals from the field at nightfall. Patricia Faust, ed., *Historical Times Illustrated Encyclopedia of the Civil War,* pp. 121 – 22.

4. A Federal regiment from Brigadier General Carl Schurz's division had crossed Freeman's Ford on a reconnaissance mission. When the Union soldiers came upon the Confederate wagon train, they sent for reinforcements and began to harass the column. Just as the additional Union troops arrived, Confederates under Brigadier General Isaac Trimble moved out to meet them. Hood's Brigade joined in the battle, and the Confederates drove off the Yankees. The field of corn was an important piece of land for the hungry Rebels, so much so that J. B. Polley's version of the battle has it precipitated by a fight between a Yankee soldier and one of the Texans over ears of corn. Davis more accurately records the action starting before the Texans came into line but also has troops from both sides gathering corn from the field. *OR,* vol. 12, pt. 2, pp. 604 – 605, 718 – 20; Davis, *Campaign from Texas to Maryland,* pp. 72 – 73; Polley, *Hood's Texas Brigade,* pp. 74 – 75; Hennessy, *Return to Bull Run,* pp. 68 – 70.

5. Campbell notes the date incorrectly here; it should be August 25.

6. Dr. R. G. Howard was a practicing physician in antebellum Houston. In October, 1861, he was acting assistant regimental surgeon. In the winter of 1861 – 62 he was ill and on furlough. He rejoined the regiment as a private in Company A through February, 1863, at which time

he is no longer in the company records. Dr. Howard survived the war and returned to his medical practice in Houston. Simpson, *Hood's Texas Brigade: A Compendium*, p. 177; Moore, "Men of the Bayou City Guards," p. 68.

7. Jubal Anderson Early was born in Virginia and schooled at West Point. Following his 1837 graduation, he fought against the Seminoles and in Mexico. As a delegate to the Virginia secession convention, Early voted against leaving the Union. Once the deed was done, though, he accepted a commission as a colonel of Virginia infantry. He was promoted to brigadier general after First Manassas; to major general in January, 1863; and to lieutenant general in May, 1864. In that year Early and the II Corps of Lee's army drove David Hunter out of the Shenandoah Valley and then marched to the outskirts of Washington, D.C. Following Lee's surrender, Early went to Mexico, then to Canada. He later returned to Virginia, taking up his law practice and becoming president of the Southern Historical Society. Early did a great deal of writing after the war, a focal point of which was a sustained attack on the reputation of James Longstreet. Davis, *Confederate General*, vol. 2, pp. 88 – 91.

8. Fitz John Porter was born in Portsmouth, New Hampshire, in 1822. He graduated from West Point in 1845 and served with distinction during the Mexican War. After the Civil War broke out, Porter was promoted to brigadier general of volunteers. He became fiercely loyal to McClellan. But he also demonstrated exceptional ability leading troops in the field during the Peninsula Campaign and Seven Days Battles. When McClellan was replaced with Pope, Porter became a vocal critic of Pope. At Second Manassas Porter was ordered to do the impossible and then brought up on charges when he failed. His trial was embroiled in politics aimed at McClellan. Porter was dismissed from the army on January 21, 1863. He dedicated himself to clearing his name, and in 1886, Pres. Grover Cleveland finally signed legislation restoring him to the army rolls. Porter died in 1901. Hubbell and Geary, *Biographical Dictionary*, pp. 412 – 13.

Chapter 8

1. Madison Monroe Templeman was an original member of Company H, 5th Texas Infantry. He was assigned to scouting duty in November, 1861. Templeman was wounded at Sharpsburg (Antietam) on September 17, 1862, and killed during a skirmish at Thoroughfare Gap, Virginia, on May 1, 1863. Simpson. *Hood's Texas Brigade: A Compendium*, p. 233.

2. The famous Chinn House, a large, wooden, two-story residence, was located almost two miles due east of the Texas Brigade's initial battle line. The Texans were embroiled in vicious fighting at the site on August 30. Hennessey, *Return to Bull Run*, p. 293 (map); Simpson, *Hood's Texas Brigade: Lee's Grenadier Guard*, pp. 145 – 58.

3. Confederate Colonel Eppa Hunton's brigade, comprising the 8th, 18th,

19th, 28th, and 56th Virginia Infantry Regiments, was positioned on the immediate right flank of the 5th Texas. About 250 yards behind Hunton and the Texans advanced Col. Montgomery Corse's brigade containing the 1st, 7th, 11th, 17th, and 24th Virginia Infantry Regiments. Hennessey, *Return to Bull Run,* pp. 388, 563.

4. William Harvey Sellers was born in Gibson County, Tennessee, in 1827. His family moved to Texas in 1835. He served as a lieutenant in a company of Texas Rangers during the Mexican War. Just prior to the start of the Civil War, Sellers returned to Texas from New York, where he had been employed as a commission merchant. The original first lieutenant of Company A, 5th Texas, Sellers was appointed adjutant general for the regiment on October 6, 1861. He then moved to brigade level, being made acting assistant adjutant general in February, 1862, and receiving the full appointment to that duty in April. Sellers later moved to the division level with Hood. Simpson, *Hood's Texas Brigade: A Compendium,* p. 5; Moore, "Men of the Bayou City Guards," pp. 18, 172.

5. John A. McMurtry was the original fourth corporal of Company A. He was promoted to third corporal, then to second corporal on November 7, 1861. After serving as regimental ordnance sergeant, McMurtry was promoted to fourth sergeant in July, 1862. He was wounded on August 30, 1862, at Second Manassas and died of his wound on November 6. Simpson, *Hood's Texas Brigade: A Compendium,* p. 174.

6. After assessing reports from several of his field commanders, Pope concluded, "Every indication during the night of the 29th and up to 10 o'clock on the morning of the 30th pointed to the retreat of the enemy from our front." *OR,* vol. 12, pt. 2, p. 41.

7. Hood was put in command of a division comprising two brigades, his own and E. M. Law's brigade, the latter consisting of the 4th Alabama, 2d and 11th Mississippi, and the 6th North Carolina Infantry Regiments. Ibid., pp. 604–606.

8. George Julius Robinson was an original private in the company. He was detached as a scout on November 22, 1861, and wounded at Gaines's Mill on June 27, 1862. Promotions to third corporal, fifth sergeant, second sergeant, and acting regimental sergeant major followed. At the Wilderness on May 6, 1864, Robinson was shot through the mouth. He was retired for disability on December 2, 1864. Simpson, *Hood's Texas Brigade: A Compendium,* p. 170.

9. Campbell may be mistaken as to the identity of the commissary officer. Harold Simpson lists no man named Gregory as a member of the 5th Texas. The regiment's commissary officer at the time was a twenty-nine-year-old bookkeeper from Ohio named Robert Burns, an original private in Campbell's company. He had been promoted to captain and appointed regimental commissary officer in May, 1862. The next year Burns was promoted to major and appointed brigade commissary officer. He surrendered with the brigade at Appomattox and after the war served with the Houston Fire Department. Ibid., p. 6; Moore, *Men of the Bayou City Guards,* pp. 27, 155.

10. Campbell refers to the 5th New York Infantry Regiment, known as

Duryee's Zouaves. They were named after the wealthy New York mer-
chant-soldier Abram Duryee, who raised the regiment in 1861 and out-
fitted the unit in colorful uniforms patterned after a French colonial
design. The New Yorkers had gained a reputation as staunch fighters
during service on the Peninsula. The assault Campbell writes about
actually occurred at midafternoon on August 30. Hennessey, *Return to
Bull Run,* pp. 366 – 73; Allen Johnson and Dumas Malone, ed., *Dictionary of American Biography,* vol. 5, p. 553.

11. The 5th New York took about 490 men into the battle. Their casualties
amounted to three officers and 76 enlisted men killed, seven officers and
163 men wounded, and 48 men captured or missing. *OR,* vol. 12, pt. 2,
pp. 260, 502 – 504.

12. After crushing the 5th New York, the Texans next struck the Pennsylvania Reserve Brigade, commanded by Col. Martin Hardin, and a battery
of Pennsylvania artillery under Capt. Mark Kerns. Hennessey, *Return to
Bull Run,* pp. 375 – 80, 556.

13. B. C. (Benjamin Charles) Simpson was born in New York about 1839 and
was a machinist before enlisting as an original member of Company A.
He was promoted to third corporal on November 7, 1861, and had risen
to third sergeant by early 1863. Simpson was wounded at Second
Manassas and later wounded and captured on July 2, 1863, at Gettysburg.
He escaped from Fort Delaware by way of Canada and returned to Houston as a crew member of a blockade runner in February, 1865. Simpson
was paroled at Houston on August 1, 1865. Afterward, he was a founding
partner of the Phoenix Iron Works in Houston. Simpson died on May 16,
1888. Simpson, *Hood's Texas Brigade: A Compendium,* p. 180; Moore, *Men
of the Bayou City Guards,* pp. 70 – 71, 174.

14. W. B. Royston was an original member of Company I, 5th Texas. He
died on September 15, 1862, of the wound he suffered at Second
Manassas. Ibid., p. 241.

15. James K. P. Harris was recruited in Virginia, enlisting on November 10,
1861. He was captured at Yorktown on May 4, 1862, and exchanged on
August 11. He died on September 20, 1862, of the wound Campbell
writes about. Ibid., p. 201.

16. The Palmetto flag was the flag of South Carolina and carried by regiments from that state, just as the Lone Star flag was carried by the
Texas regiments.

17. The Texans intermixed with soldiers from the Hampton Legion, the
18th Georgia Infantry, and several Virginia regiments from Corse's and
Hunton's brigades. *OR,* vol. 12, pt. 2, pp. 617 – 22; Hennessey, *Return
to Bull Run,* pp. 378 – 90, 563.

18. Henry Lewis Benning was born in Columbia County, Georgia, in 1814.
He was an 1834 graduate of Franklin College (now the University of
Georgia), a lawyer, and an associate justice of the Georgia Supreme
Court. Benning entered the war in August, 1861, as colonel of the 17th
Georgia Infantry, a regiment that he himself raised. He eventually at-
tained the rank of brigadier general, having served with distinction in
nearly all the battles fought by the Army of Northern Virginia. At the

Battle of Second Manassas, Colonel Benning was commanding Brig. Gen. Robert Toombs's brigade, comprising the 2d, 15th, 17th, and 20th Georgia Regiments, in the general's absence. At the point in the battle described by Campbell, Benning had gone to the area occupied by the 20th Georgia to evaluate the situation, and he subsequently led them in the attack. Davis, *Confederate General,* vol. 1, pp. 100 – 101 *OR,* vol. 19, pt. 1, pp. 888 – 93.

Chapter 9

1. James Downey was an original member of Company A. He performed extra duty as a regimental saddler beginning on January 9, 1862. In 1863 he was detailed as a litter bearer. While the regiment was in Tennessee after the Chickamauga and Knoxville Campaigns, Downey was detailed as a shoemaker. He was wounded at Chaffin's Farm on September 27, 1864, and again at Darbytown Road on October 7, 1864. He was paroled during the surrender at Appomattox. Simpson, *Hood's Texas Brigade: A Compendium,* p. 176.
2. F. Charles Hume was the original fourth corporal of Company D, 5th Texas. He was assigned to scouting duty on November 22, 1861. Hume was wounded near Richmond on June 8, 1862, and at Second Manassas on August 30. He transferred to the 32d Virginia Cavalry on December 7, 1862. Ibid., p.197.
3. Although the 5th Texas did indeed suffer more casualties than any other regiment in the entire Army of Northern Virginia during the Battle of Second Manassas (15 killed, 224 wounded, according to the report of the army's medical director, Surgeon Lafayette Guild), official reports indicate Campbell's figures are too high. In addition to the surgeon's report, Col. J. B. Robertson reported the casualties for the regiment as 15 killed, 245 wounded and 1 missing. Both the 18th Georgia (19 killed, 114 wounded) and the 4th Texas (22 killed, 77 wounded) suffered more losses than the Hampton Legion (11 killed, 63 wounded). *OR,* vol. 12, pt. 2, pp. 560, 619; Hennessey, *Return to Bull Run,* p. 405.
4. On September 4, 1862, the Army of Northern Virginia crossed the Potomac River into Maryland, embarking on its first invasion of Northern territory. Two weeks later Lee's battered army slipped back over the river into Virginia following the brutal Battle of Sharpsburg (Antietam), the bloodiest single day of combat of the entire war. Faust, *Encyclopedia,* pp. 19 – 20.
5. R. J. Breckinridge was appointed regimental surgeon on November 8, 1861. He had an assignment with the Army Medical Board in Richmond in March, 1862, and was made chief medical inspector of the Army of Northern Virginia in the fall of that year. Simpson, *Hood's Texas Brigade: A Compendium,* p. 168.
6. John Cabell Breckinridge was born near Lexington, Kentucky, in 1821. He studied and practiced law in Kentucky and quickly entered the national political arena. In 1856 Breckinridge was elected vice president of the United States. He left that position to assume the U.S. Senate

seat from Kentucky. Breckinridge opposed the war but accepted a brigadier's commission with the Confederacy, serving in both the western and eastern theaters. After the Confederacy's surrender, Breckinridge went to Europe, then Canada. He returned to Kentucky and his law practice in 1869 and lived there until his death in 1875. Davis, *Confederate General*, vol. 1, pp. 126 – 27.

7. Samuel Bailey, born in Alabama, was a twenty-three-year-old stable keeper when he enlisted as an original member of the company. He was wounded on June 27, 1862, at Gaines's Mill, then wounded in two places and captured on August 30, 1862, at Second Manassas. After being exchanged, Bailey was wounded again at Gettysburg on July 2, 1863. On May 10, 1864, Bailey was killed at Spotsylvania, suffering a particularly gruesome fate. An artillery shot removed his head from his body, scattering pieces upon his comrades, and drove his weapon through a nearby soldier. Simpson, *Hood's Texas Brigade: A Compendium*, p. 174; *Hood's Texas Brigade: Lee's Grenadier Guard*, p. 413; Moore, *Men of the Bayou City Guards*, pp. 86 – 87, 153.

8. J. S. Norton was a thirty-one-year-old merchant from Connecticut when he enlisted as an original private in the company. He was appointed regimental hospital steward and then detailed to the ambulance corps in April, 1862. He was captured at Second Manassas, August 30, 1862, and paroled on November 14. Norton served later in the war as a regimental musician. He left the unit on furlough in April, 1864, and never returned. Norton was paroled in North Carolina on May 22, 1865. Simpson, *Hood's Texas Brigade: A Compendium*, p. 171; Moore, *Men of the Bayou City Guards*, p. 169.

9. James E. Landes was an original member of Company A. On May 6, 1864, he was wounded at the Wilderness, losing a finger. Landes was paroled during the surrender at Appomattox. Simpson, *Hood's Texas Brigade: A Compendium*, p. 177.

10. Campbell is probably referring to James R. Netherly, who was recruited about the same time as Campbell. Born in Alabama, Netherly was a thirty-three-year-old carpenter at the time of his enlistment. He was wounded at Malvern Hill on July 1, 1862, and died at Warrenton, Virginia, on October 4, 1862, of chronic diarrhea. Simpson, *Hood's Texas Brigade: A Compendium*, p. 179; Moore, *Men of the Bayou City Guards*, p. 169.

11. The *Roster of Confederate Soldiers* lists three assistant surgeons with the last name Crow and initials N. J. Campbell's N. J. Crow probably served with the 42d Virginia Infantry, which was at Second Manassas. Another N. J. Crow served with the 62d Virginia Mounted Infantry, a unit not present at Manassas. N. Jefferson Crow is the third possibility but is listed as a staff officer. Janet B. Hewett, *Roster of Confederate Soldiers*, vol. 4, p. 27; *OR*, vol. 12, pt. 2, pp. 546 – 51.

12. Arthur H. Edey maintained an office in Richmond from which he acted on behalf of the men of the Texas Brigade. Through his office, mail and creature comforts were sent to the troops and news from the front was sent back home. In his letter printed on this date, Edey promised to

"ascertain and answer any enquiries respecting the safety and health of this command." He wrote that anyone traveling with letters for the soldiers could leave them at his office, and he would see that they were delivered. Edey also asked that those people stop in his office before their return to Texas so they could carry letters back from the soldiers. *Houston Tri-Weekly Telegraph,* Sept. 8, 1862, p. 2.

13. Campbell probably is referring again to James Netherly.

14. This may be John Hefferan, another of the recruits from March, 1862. Hefferan was thirty at the time of his enlistment. He died of a jaw wound suffered at Second Manassas. Simpson, *Hood's Texas Brigade: A Compendium,* p. 177; Moore, *Men of the Bayou City Guards,* p. 163.

15. John De Young was eighteen years old when he enlisted with the same group as Campbell. Simpson, *Hood's Texas Brigade: A Compendium,* p. 176; Moore, *Men of the Bayou City Guards,* p. 159.

16. Albert Angel was twenty-four years old when he enlisted on March 14, 1862. He died on September 5, 1862, following amputation of a leg due to a thigh wound suffered at Second Manassas on August 30. Simpson, *Hood's Texas Brigade: A Compendium,* p. 174; Moore, *Men of the Bayou City Guards,* p. 153.

17. John N. Massenburg of Virginia was twenty-three years old when recruited on March 22, 1862, in Harris County, Texas. He died of a thigh wound at Second Manassas. Simpson, *Hood's Texas Brigade: A Compendium,* p. 178; Moore, *Men of the Bayou City Guards,* p. 167.

18. Nurses at the time of the Civil War were usually males. The female nurses that did tend to the wounded came from private aid agencies or acted on their own.

19. Col. W. H. Payne, 4th Virginia Cavalry, had charge of a company at Warrenton, his duties including protection of public property. He had command in Warrenton as early as May 8, 1861. Payne still had command there on October 22, 1862. Official records give no information to back up Campbell's claim that Payne was captured in Warrenton in September, 1862. *OR,* vol. 2, p. 819; vol. 19, pt. 2, pp. 676, 697–98.

20. S. D. Hewes, born on December 11, 1824, was a sawmill manager and "speculator" from Pennsylvania. An original member of the company, he was assigned duty as a sawmill supervisor for a short time in 1861. The next year he went on the recruiting trip that brought Campbell to the unit. Wounded at Second Manassas on August 30, 1862, Hewes was furloughed and then discharged due to disability on June 15, 1863. Simpson, *Hood's Texas Brigade: A Compendium,* p. 177; Moore, *Men of the Bayou City Guards,* p. 153.

21. J. R. Patton was thirty years old when he signed up on March 12, 1862. He suffered a wound at Second Manassas on August 30, 1862. He died of smallpox the following spring. Simpson, *Hood's Texas Brigade: A Compendium,* p. 179; Moore, *Men of the Bayou City Guards,* p. 170.

22. A. G. Monell enlisted on March 29, 1862, at the age of twenty-seven. He went AWOL during the autumn of 1862 and was subsequently declared a deserter. Simpson, *Hood's Texas Brigade: A Compendium,* p. 178; Moore, *Men of the Bayou City Guards,* p. 168.

NOTES TO PAGES 85–89

23. Campbell may again have confused the name of William B. Ferrell, who was assigned to the Texas Brigade hospital at this time. Simpson does not list in his *Compendium* a Jas. Farrell as a member of the company.

24. Prisoner-of-war exchanges were common at this stage of the conflict. Such arrangements stipulated that the captive did not return to active duty until exchanged for an enemy prisoner of similar rank. The practice was halted later in the war. Faust, *Encyclopedia*, p. 558.

25. R. Gaston Ashe, who is thought to have been born in 1842, was a Harris County resident. He enlisted in Company B, Terry's Texas Rangers (8th Texas Cavalry), in Houston in September, 1861, but was discharged in April, 1862. Sometime later Ashe married Sallie Jones, and the couple had at least one son. "R. Gaston Ashe," *The Online Archives of Terry's Texas Rangers;* "Mary (Smith McCrory) Jones Collection 1858-1900," *University of Houston Libraries Special Collections Guides.*

26. The Terry Rangers were a cavalry regiment given the formal designation of the 8th Texas Cavalry. The regiment was organized in Houston in 1861.

27. Thomas Harrison was born in Alabama on May 1, 1823. His family moved to Mississippi when he was a child. Harrison moved back and forth between Mississippi and Texas a couple of times, going to Houston in the late 1840s and then to Waco in 1855. Early in the war he commanded a company of cavalry in Terry's Texas Rangers. Harrison rose to command that unit and later led a brigade. He was wounded at Monroe's Crossroads, North Carolina, on March 10, 1865. Harrison returned to Waco after the war and died there on July 14, 1891. Davis, *Confederate General*, vol. 3, pp. 70 – 71.

28. Joseph T. Cobb was a private in Company G, 6th Texas Cavalry. "Joseph T. Cobb," *Civil War Soldiers and Sailors System Search Detail.*

29. Meriwether Jefferson Thompson was born in Virginia in 1826. Before the war he had been mayor of St. Joseph, Missouri. As the secession issue heated up, Thompson became an officer in the pro-Southern Missouri State Guard. He was a brigadier general in the guard by the first summer of the war. In that position he commanded Confederate troops on raiding parties in Missouri. Later in the summer of 1862, Thompson commanded Confederate troops operating near New Orleans. He returned to the Arkansas-Missouri area in 1863 and was captured. Exchanged in 1864, Thompson again commanded troops in the West. He surrendered on May 11, 1865. Sifakis, *Who Was Who in the Confederacy,* p. 280.

30. R. B. Jarmon was a private in Company F, 1st Texas Infantry. He enlisted on July 9, 1861, in Richmond. For much of 1862, Jarmon was hospitalized. When he returned to duty, Jarmon served in the army intelligence office, brigade headquarters, and the medical board office. Simpson, *Hood's Texas Brigade: A Compendium,* p. 47.

Appendix A. Letters and Other Writings

1. The loss of the Texas Brigade at Gaines's Mill amounted to 86 killed, 481 wounded, and 4 captured, a total of 571. *OR*, vol. 11, pt. 2, p. 973.

2. Nathan Bedford Forrest was an aggressive cavalry commander and a formidable fighter. Born on July 13, 1821, in Tennessee, he was a successful businessman before the Civil War. Forrest began his service as a private but was quickly discharged and authorized to raise a battalion of mounted rangers. Several times during the conflict Forrest would reorganize units or raise a command from scratch and make it an effective fighting force. By the end of the war, he had attained the rank of lieutenant general, personally killed or seriously wounded at least thirty of the enemy, and been wounded himself four times. The accomplished general was not able to duplicate his success in business after the war. Forrest died on October 29, 1877. Davis, *Confederate General*, vol. 2, pp. 138 – 45.

3. John Gregg was born in Alabama on September 28, 1828. He practiced law and politics in Texas before the war and was a delegate to the state's secession convention. Gregg represented Texas in the Confederate Congress but gave up his seat to recruit a regiment. He fought in the western theater, rising to command of a brigade, until being reassigned to Lt. Gen. James Longstreet's corps and the command of Hood's Texas Brigade in the spring of 1864. Gregg's life ended in combat on the Charles City Road near Richmond on October 7, 1864. By then he had distinguished himself as a tough fighter and respected leader. Ibid., vol. 3, pp. 36 – 39.

4. This was the division commanded by Maj. Gen. William Henry Talbot Walker. Born in Augusta, Georgia, on November 26, 1816, Walker was an 1837 West Point graduate. He fought in the Seminole wars in Florida and in the Mexican War and was seriously wounded in each conflict. Walker was commissioned a brigadier general in the Confederate Army prior to First Manassas. He resigned, citing poor health, in October, 1861, but returned to service in March, 1863. On July 22, 1864, Walker was unjustly criticized by Lieutenant General William Hardee for his actions during a march to strike at Union forces near Atlanta. Hardee later apologized, but Walker's life had ended soon after the incident when he was shot by a Federal soldier. *OR*, vol. 30, pt. 2, p. 14; Davis, *Confederate General*, vol. 6, pp. 98 – 99.

5. On the card containing Campbell's information from the bimonthly company muster roll for the period of January – February, 1864, he is listed as having been detailed as a courier with brigade headquarters on February 27, 1864. Cards for the following months through August, 1864, carry the same information. The card for September – October, 1864, notes that Campbell was absent at that time due to a wound suffered on October 7, 1864. *Compiled Service Records of Confederate Soldiers Who Served in Organizations from Texas.*

6. R. A. Curtis was a sergeant in Company L, 1st Texas Infantry. Reuben T. Crigler was a lieutenant with Company F, 4th Texas Infantry and

was wounded at the Wilderness. Campbell was still carried on the rolls of Company A, 5th Texas Infantry. Robert B. Clyde was in the 3d Arkansas band and was listed as ill for most of 1863. He may not have been with the brigade at the Wilderness. R. A. H. Caldeleugh was a private in Company A, 3d Arkansas Infantry. Simpson, *Hood's Texas Brigade: A Compendium*. pp. 80, 131, 175, 256, 260.

7. Edward A. Pollard, a Virginian and the wartime editor of the *Richmond Examiner*, published *The Lost Cause: A New Southern History of the War of the Confederates* in 1866. His stated intent was to write an honest and objective history of the war. What he produced is a glorification of the antebellum Southern way of life and the noble Southern soldier and a repudiation of what he considers the decadent North. Pollard also takes to task Jefferson Davis and the Confederate government, attributing the ultimate blame for the loss of the war to bad leadership. He closes his book with the assertions that the Confederates came out of the war knowing they were "THE BETTER MEN" and that the possibility remained that in time the South would attain its rightful position of superiority. *The Lost Cause* set a tone for those who wished to see in the South something other than what had resulted from four years of civil war.

8. Lafayette McLaws was born on January 15, 1821, in Augusta, Georgia. He was an 1842 graduate of West Point and slowly rose to the rank of captain in the U.S. Army. McLaws began the Civil War as a major in the Confederate service but attained the rank of brigadier general by September, 1861, and major general by May, 1862. He initially had a strong supporter in Lt. Gen. James Longstreet, but his critical comments on Longstreet's behavior at Gettysburg were met by court-martial charges after Knoxville. McLaws ended the war participating in the defense of the East Coast. He died in Savannah on July 24, 1897. Davis, *Confederate General*, vol. 4, pp. 128 – 31.

9. Braxton Bragg was born at Warrenton, North Carolina, on March 22, 1817. He graduated from West Point in 1837 and served with distinction in the Mexican War. It was there that he began a friendship with the future president of the Confederacy, Jefferson Davis. Bragg's inability to get along with fellow officers led to his resignation from the U.S. Army in 1856. In 1860 the governor of Louisiana appointed Bragg to a board to organize an army for the state, and when secession came Bragg was put at the head of that army. Although a good organizer, several times Bragg let success slip away and frequently fought with his subordinates. His greatest victory was at Chickamauga, but even there he failed to follow up. After the war Bragg worked as an engineer until his death on September 27, 1876. Ibid., vol. 1, pp. 112 – 17.

10. Charles William Field was born on April 6, 1828, in Kentucky. He was a West Point graduate, class of 1849. Successful early on as a field commander of Virginia troops, a serious wound suffered at Second Manassas put Field behind a desk until 1864, when he was assigned command of Hood's division. Field surrendered at Appomattox and died exactly twenty-seven years later on April 9, 1892. Ibid., vol. 2, pp. 124 – 25.

11. Joseph Brevard Kershaw was born on January 5, 1822, at Camden, South Carolina. Before the Civil War he was a lawyer, a legislator, and a volunteer in the Mexican War. Kershaw's troops played key roles in many Confederate successes. On April 6, 1865, his command was finally overwhelmed, with many soldiers, including Kershaw, being captured at Sayler's Creek. Following the war, Kershaw returned to the practice of law and politics. He died on April 13, 1894. Ibid., vol. 4, pp. 10 – 13.

12. Gregg's reference was to the battle of December 5, 1805, in which Napoleon's outnumbered troops won a major victory over the forces allied against him. As the battle began, a heavy fog lifted, replaced by a brilliant sun. To Gregg, commanding the outnumbered Confederates, the rising sun must have seemed a good omen.

13. Cadmus Marcellus Wilcox was born in North Carolina. He struggled at West Point, but graduated with the class of 1846. Wilcox served well in Mexico and wrote well-received historical and technical works, aided by that experience. He left the U.S. Army when Tennessee left the Union and began Confederate service as the colonel of the 9th Alabama Infantry. Wilcox established a good combat record throughout the war, earning promotion to command of a division. He died in Washington, D.C., on December 2, 1890. Davis, *Confederate General*, vol. 6, pp. 138 – 41.

14. Campbell refers to Maj. Gen. Henry Heth, a Virginia-born graduate of the West Point class of 1847. Heth struggled early in the war during action in western Virginia. But in January, 1863, he was transferred to the Army of Northern Virginia, where he was promoted to command of a division. He gained everlasting fame when his troops collided with Federal forces at Gettysburg, thus precipitating a major battle that his commander was not ready for. Heth served capably, for the most part, until the end of the war. His later years were marked by ill health, and he died in 1899. Ibid., vol. 3, pp. 88 – 91.

15. Richard Heron Anderson was born in South Carolina on October 7, 1821. After graduation from West Point in 1842, Anderson served in the U.S. Army until March 3, 1861; two weeks later he was commissioned a major in the Confederate cavalry. After serving in South Carolina and Florida, Anderson joined the Army of Northern Virginia on January 31, 1862. When Longstreet was wounded at the Wilderness on May 7, 1864, Anderson was put in command of the I Corps until the latter's return. The war ended for Anderson when his command was destroyed at Sayler's Creek. He died in South Carolina on June 26, 1879. Ibid., vol. 1, pp. 28 – 29.

16. Benjamin Grubb Humphreys was born in 1808 in Mississippi, where he became a planter and politician. Opposed to secession, he still followed his state out of the Union and raised a company. As the war went on, Humphreys repeatedly arrived with his men at the right place at the right time. He was promoted to brigadier general after Gettysburg and continued to provide excellent combat service until being wounded on September 3, 1864. Humphreys died at his plantation on December 20, 1882. Ibid., vol. 3, pp. 132 – 33.

17. Leonard Gee was an original member of Company E, 5th Texas. He was ill in Winchester late in 1862. In October, 1863, Gee was assigned to be a courier for the brigade staff. He was wounded in the arm at the Wilderness on May 6, 1864, and furloughed to Mississippi. Simpson, *Hood's Texas Brigade: A Compendium,* p. 206.

18. Reports of casualties for the brigade vary and no official report is known to exist. All accounts indicate the casualties were extremely high. For a discussion of the Texas Brigade casualty figures, see Simpson, *Hood's Texas Brigade: Lee's Grenadier Guard.*

19. Moore, "Men of the Bayou City Guards," p. 145.

20. William Starke Rosecrans was born in Ohio on September 6, 1819. A West Point graduate, he left the service to work as a civil engineer. When the war started, Rosecrans was brought back into the Regular Army as a brigadier general. He enjoyed a good deal of success campaigning in the western theater, but that came to an end with his defeat at Chickamauga. Rosecrans led an active life after the war, culminating in a seat in Congress from California. He died in California on March 11, 1898. Hubbell and Geary, *Biographical Dictionary,* pp. 444–45.

21. Ambrose Everett Burnside was born on May 23, 1824, in Indiana. He was a West Point graduate but left the military in 1853. Burnside reentered the army at the start of the Civil War, commanding Rhode Island troops. He served in a series of high positions during the war and proved unequal to the task in most of them, his resistance to Longstreet's siege of Knoxville being a notable exception. After the war Burnside enjoyed better success in business and politics. He died on September 13, 1881. Ibid., pp. 74–75.

22. Ulysses Simpson Grant, born Hiram Ulysses Grant at Point Pleasant, Ohio, on April 27, 1822, struggled through life whenever he had to survive as a businessman but excelled when he had to make war. The success bred by his unrelenting nature as a fighter prompted his promotion to general in chief of the Federal armies, and his campaign with the Army of the Potomac in 1864–65 ultimately wore down the Army of Northern Virginia. Military success in turn led to a troubled presidency, but at the end of his life, Grant achieved a literary triumph with his memoirs. He died on July 23, 1885. William S. McFeely, *Grant: A Biography.*

23. Pierre Gustave Toutant Beauregard was born on May 28, 1818, near New Orleans. Inspired by his study of Napoleon, he attended West Point and graduated second in his 1838 class. While serving with the engineers during the Mexican War, Beauregard earned brevet promotion to the rank of major. He received an appointment as a brigadier general in the Confederate Army dated March 1, 1861. Beauregard commanded victorious forces at First Manassas and subsequently was promoted to full general. But he soon began bickering with the Confederate government and developed an animosity that was reciprocated by Jefferson Davis throughout the war. After being removed from field command by Davis, Beauregard orchestrated a defense of Charleston, and later his troops in North Carolina shielded Robert E. Lee's army

and Richmond. Beauregard enjoyed business success after the war and
died in New Orleans on February 20, 1893. Davis, *Confederate General*,
vol. 1, pp. 84 – 93.

24. Campbell refers to the Battle of the Crater. Union soldiers with a coal
mining background had tunneled under a Confederate fortification and
set off an explosive charge. Federal troops followed up the blast with an
assault. They were stunned by the sight of the results of the explosion,
failed to press the attack, and were trapped in the crater by Confederate
reinforcements. The Federals made easy targets for the Rebel troops
firing into the pit from the rim. The original plan had been for black
troops to make the charge, but a last-minute change had the black soldiers coming in behind white troops. Nonetheless, the black soldiers
were caught in the chaos inside the crater and suffered heavy casualties.
Jeff Kinard, *The Battle of the Crater.*

25. Fort Pillow was a Union fortification on a bluff overlooking the Mississippi River in Tennessee. It was manned by white soldiers from Tennessee and a large contingent of black troops. Confederate forces led by
Maj. Gen. Nathan Bedford Forrest attacked in April, 1864, driving the
Federals from the fort and inflicting heavy casualties. Afterward the
North charged that the Confederates had massacred wounded and surrendered soldiers, a claim that Forrest denied. Richard L. Fuchs, *An
Unerring Fire: The Massacre at Fort Pillow;* Faust, *Encyclopedia,* pp.
277 – 78.

26. Confederate lieutenant general Jubal Early had taken a force into the
Shenandoah Valley in the spring of 1864. He defeated Major General
David Hunter's command and then marched toward Washington, D.C.
A delaying action at the Monocacy River by troops under Major General Lew Wallace stalled Early's march just long enough to allow reinforcements to man the defenses around Washington, leaving Early
close enough indeed to serenade "Old Abe" but unable to do much
more. The Confederates returned to the Shenandoah Valley, where
they were defeated by Major General Phil Sheridan at Cedar Creek.
Meanwhile in Georgia, Union major general William T. Sherman was
encircling the city of Atlanta, all the while engaging Confederate forces
in battle. By September 3, the city was in Federal hands. Frank
Vandiver, *Jubal's Raid: General Early's Famous Attack on Washington in
1864;* James Lee McDonough and James Pickett Jones, *"War So
Terrible": Sherman and Atlanta.*

27. John Clifford Pemberton was born on August 10, 1814, in Philadelphia.
He was an 1837 West Point graduate and a veteran of the Mexican War.
As a lieutenant general, Pemberton commanded the defenses of Vicksburg until he surrendered the city and its garrison on July 4, 1863. With
no position available for him at that rank, Pemberton resigned his commission, and Jefferson Davis subsequently appointed him a lieutenant
colonel in the artillery, which he retained until the end of the war. After
the war Pemberton lived on a Virginia farm and later moved back to his
home state, where he died on July 13, 1881. Davis, *Confederate General*,
vol. 5, pp. 8 – 9.

28. King Bryan began the war as captain of Company F, 5th Texas. He was wounded at Second Manassas on August 30, 1862, and promoted to major effective that date. On November 1, he was promoted to lieutenant colonel. Bryan was wounded two more times, at Gettysburg on July 2, 1863, and at the Wilderness on May 6, 1864. Simpson, *Hood's Texas Brigade: A Compendium*, p. 167.

29. John I. Shotwell was an original third lieutenant of Company B, 1st Texas and rose to the rank of captain. He held a number of special positions, including detached service with the division provost guard, acting inspector general for the brigade, and acting aide-de-camp to General Gregg. In December, 1864, he was transferred to the "Foreign Battalion," raised by Maj. Garnett Andrews. Ibid., p. 20.

30. Winkler, *Confederate Capital*, pp. 234–35.

31. A corporal's guard is the relatively few men needed to man sentinel posts in a camp or base. It would consist of a small number of privates commanded by a corporal.

32. Thomas McKinney Jack was born at San Felipe de Austin, Texas, on December 19, 1831. After graduating with honors from Yale in 1835, he practiced law in Texas. When that state seceded, Jack volunteered as an aide to Col. Sidney Sherman. He took part in a number of western-theater battles. On June 14, 1864, Jack was promoted to colonel. After being transferred to the Trans-Mississippi Department, he was named adjutant general of Texas. Jack returned to practicing law after the war. He died on August 26, 1880. "Thomas McKinney Jack," *Handbook of Texas Online*.

BIBLIOGRAPHY

Allan, Francis D., comp. *Allan's Lone Star Ballads: A Collection of Southern Patriotic Songs Made during Confederate Times.* Galveston: J. D. Sawyer, 1874. Reprint, New York: Burt Franklin, 1970.

Andrews, J. Cutler. *The South Reports the Civil War.* Princeton: Princeton University Press, 1970. Reprint, Pittsburgh: University of Pittsburgh Press, 1985.

"Ashe, R. Gaston." *The Online Archives of Terry's Texas Rangers.* June 6, 2002 < http://terrystexasrangers.org/roster/a/ashe_rg.htm >.

Barziza, Decimus et Ultimus. *The Adventures of a Prisoner of War.* 1865. Reprint, Austin: University of Texas Press, 1964.

Battles and Leaders of the Civil War. 4 vols. New York: Thomas Yoseloff, 1956.

Bowers, John. *Chickamauga and Chattanooga: The Battles That Doomed the Confederacy.* New York: Harper Collins, 1994.

———. *Stonewall Jackson: Portrait of a Soldier.* New York: William Morrow, 1989.

Callahan, Martin L. "Returned with Honor: The Flag of the 5th Texas." *North South Trader's Civil War* 25, no.2 (March – April, 1998): 36 – 42.

Coates, Earl J., and Dean S. Thomas. *An Introduction to Civil War Small Arms.* Gettysburg, Penn.: Thomas, 1990.

"Cobb, Joseph T." *Civil War Soldiers & Sailors System Search Detail.* June 9, 2002 < http://www.itd.nps.gov/cwss/soldiers.htm >.

Collier, Calvin. *They'll Do to Tie To: The Story of the Third Regiment, Arkansas Infantry, C.S.A.* Little Rock: Pioneer, 1959.

Commager, Henry Steele, ed. *The Blue and the Gray: The Story of the Civil War as Told by the Participants.* Indianapolis: Bobbs-Merrill, 1950.

Compiled Service Records of Confederate Soldiers Who Served in Organizations from Texas. National Archives, Washington, D.C. Photocopy.

Cooling, B. Franklin. *Forts Henry and Donelson: The Key to the Confederate Heartland.* Knoxville: University of Tennessee Press, 1987.

Cozzens, Peter. *This Terrible Sound: The Battle of Chickamauga.* Urbana: University of Illinois Press, 1996.

Cullen, Joseph P. *The Peninsula Campaign, 1862.* Harrisburg, Penn.: Stackpole Books, 1973.

Dabney, Virginius. *Richmond: The Story of a City.* Garden City, N.Y.: Doubleday, 1976.

Davis, Nicholas A. *The Campaign from Texas to Maryland with the Battle of Fredericksburg.* Richmond: Office of the Presbyterian Committee of Publication of the Confederate States, 1863. Reprint, Austin: Steck, 1961.

Davis, William C., ed. *The Confederate General.* 6 vols. Harrisburg, Penn.: National Historical Society, 1991.

Dickison, J. J. *Military History of Florida.* Vol. 16 of *Confederate Military History.* Confederate Publishing, 1899. Reprint, Wilmington, N.C.: Broadfoot, 1989.

DiNardo, R. L., and Albert A. Nofi, eds. *James Longstreet: The Man, the Soldier, the Controversy.* Conshohocken, Penn.: Combined, 1998.

Dowdey, Clifford. *The Seven Days: The Emergence of Lee.* Boston: Little, Brown, 1964.

Dyer, John P. *The Gallant Hood.* Indianapolis: Bobbs-Merrill, 1950. Reprint, Old Saybrook, Conn.: Konecky and Konecky, 1993.

Farwell, Byron. *Stonewall: A Biography of General Thomas J. Jackson.* New York: W. W. Norton, 1992.

Faust, Patricia, ed. *Historical Times Illustrated Encyclopedia of the Civil War.* New York: Harper and Row, 1986.

Fehrenbach, T. R. *Lone Star: A History of Texas and the Texans.* New York: Macmillan, 1968.

Fleming, Elvis E. "Some Hard Fighting: Letters of Private Robert T. Wilson, 5th Texas Infantry, Hood's Brigade, 1862 – 1864." *Military History of Texas and the Southwest* 9 (1971): 289 – 302.

Fletcher, William Andrew. *Rebel Private, Front and Rear.* Beaumont, Tex.: Press of the Greer Print, 1908. Reprint, Washington, D.C.: Zenger, 1985.

Freeman, Douglas Southall. *Lee's Lieutenants: A Study in Command.* 3 vols. New York: Charles Scribner's Sons, 1942 – 44.

——. *R. E. Lee: A Biography.* 4 vols. New York: Charles Scribner's Sons, 1934.

Fuchs, Richard L. *An Unerring Fire: The Massacre at Fort Pillow.* London: Associated University Presses, 1994.

Gallagher, Gary W., ed. *Lee: The Soldier.* Lincoln: University of Nebraska Press, 1996.

——. *The Richmond Campaign of 1862: The Peninsula and the Seven Days.* Chapel Hill: University of North Carolina Press, 2000.

——. *The Wilderness Campaign.* Chapel Hill: University of North Carolina Press, 1997.

Giles, Val C. *Rags and Hope: The Recollections of Val C. Giles, Four Years with Hood's Brigade, Fourth Texas Infantry, 1861–1865.* New York: Coward-McCann, 1961.

Harsh, Joseph L. *Taken at the Flood: Robert E. Lee and Confederate Strategy in the Maryland Campaign of 1862.* Kent, Ohio: The Kent State University Press, 1999.

Hastings, Earl C., Jr.; and David S. Hastings. *A Pitiless Rain: The Battle of Williamsburg, 1862.* Shippensburg, Penn.: White Mane, 1997.

Hennessy, John J. *Return to Bull Run: The Campaign and Battle of Second Manassas.* New York: Touchstone, 1994.

Hewett, Janet B., ed. *The Roster of Confederate Soldiers 1861–1865.* 10 vols. Wilmington, N.C.: Broadfoot, 1996.

Hood, John Bell. *Advance and Retreat: Personal Experiences in the United States and Confederate Armies.* New Orleans: For Hood Memorial Fund by P. G. T. Beauregard, 1880. Reprint, with a new introduction by Richard M. McMurry, New York: Da Capo, 1993.

Houston Chronicle. June 25, 1924. S. O. Young Collection, Houston Metropolitan Research Center.

Houston News Bulletin. 1864 – 65. Eugene C. Barker Texas History Center, The University of Texas at Austin. Microfilm.

Houston Telegraph Extras. 1861 – 63. Eugene C. Barker Texas History Center, The University of Texas at Austin. Microfilm.

Houston Tri-Weekly Telegraph. 1861 – 65. Eugene C. Barker Texas History Center, The University of Texas at Austin. Microfilm.

Houston Weekly Telegraph. 1861 – 65. Eugene C. Barker Texas History Center, The University of Texas at Austin. Microfilm.

Hubbell, John T., and James W. Geary, ed. *Biographical Dictionary of the Union: Northern Leaders of the Civil War.* Westport, Conn.: Greenwood, 1995.

Hudson, Leonne M., *The Odyssey of a Southerner: The Life and Times of Gustavus Woodson Smith.* Macon, Ga.: Mercer University Press, 1998.

"Jack, Thomas McKinney." *The Handbook of Texas Online.* January 19, 2002 < http://www.tsha.utexas.edu/handbook/online/articles/view/JJ/fja3.html >.

Johnson, Allan, and Dumas Malone, ed. *Dictionary of American Biography.* New York: Charles Scribner's Sons, 1930.

Jones, Katharine M. *Ladies of Richmond: Confederate Capital.* Indianapolis: Bobbs-Merrill, 1962.

Jones, Tom. *Tom Jones' Hood's Texas Brigade Sketch Book.* Hillsboro, Tex.: Hill College Press, 1988.

Kelley, Dayton. *General Lee and Hood's Texas Brigade at the Battle of the Wilderness.* Hillsboro, Tex.: Hill Junior College Press, 1969.

Kinard, Jeff. *The Battle of the Crater.* Fort Worth: Ryan Place, 1995.

King, Alvy L. *Louis T. Wigfall, Southern Fire-eater.* Baton Rouge: Louisiana State University Press, 1970.

Krick, Robert K. *Lee's Colonels: A Biographical Register of the Field Officers of the Army of Northern Virginia.* 4th ed., rev. Dayton, Ohio: Morningside, 1992.

Longstreet, James. *From Manassas to Appomattox: Memoirs of the Civil War in America.* Philadelphia: J. B. Lippincott, 1896.

Marlin (Tex.) Daily Democrat. June 26, 1903. S. O. Young Collection, Houston Metropolitan Research Center.

Martin, David G. *The Peninsula Campaign, March–July, 1862.* Conshohocken, Penn.: Combined Books, 1992.

———. *The Second Bull Run Campaign, July–August, 1862.* Conshohocken, Penn.: Combined Books, 1997.

"Mary (Smith McCrory) Jones Collection 1858 – 1900." *University of Houston Libraries Special Collections Guides.* June 6, 2002 < http://info.lib.uh.edu/speccoll/guides/jones.htm >.

McCarthy, Carlton. *Detailed Minutiae of Soldier Life in the Army of Northern Virginia, 1861–1865.* Richmond: Carlton McCarthy, 1882. Reprint, Lincoln: University of Nebraska Press, 1993.

McClellan, H. B. *The Life and Campaigns of Major-General J. E. B. Stuart, Commander of the Cavalry of the Army of Northern Virginia.* Secaucus, N.J.: Blue and Gray, 1993.

McDonough, James Lee, and James Pickett Jones. *"War So Terrible": Sherman and Atlanta.* New York: W. W. Norton, 1987.

McFeely, William S. *Grant: A Biography.* New York: W. W. Norton, 1981.

McMurry, Richard M. *John Bell Hood and the War for Southern Independence.* Lexington: University Press of Kentucky, 1982.

Miller, William J., ed. *The Peninsula Campaign of 1862: Yorktown to the Seven Days.* Campbell, Calif.: Savas Woodbury, 1997.

Moore, James Orville. "The Men of the Bayou City Guards (Company A, 5th Texas Infantry, Hood's Brigade)." Master's thesis, University of Houston – Clear Lake, 1988.

Newton, Steven H. *Joseph E. Johnston and the Defense of Richmond.* Lawrence: University Press of Kansas, 1998.

Parker, Eddy R., ed. *Touched by Fire: Letters from Company D, 5th Texas Infantry, Hood's Brigade, Army of Northern Virginia, 1862–1865.* Hillsboro, Tex.: Hill College Press, 2000.

Polley, J. B. *Hood's Texas Brigade: Its Marches, Its Battles, Its Achievements.* New York: Neale, 1910. Reprint, Dayton, Ohio: Morningside, 1988.

———. *A Soldier's Letters to Charming Nellie.* New York: Neale, 1908. Reprint, Gaithersburg, Md.: Butternut, 1984.

Powell, Robert M. *Recollections of a Texas Colonel at Gettysburg.* Edited by Gregory A. Coco. Gettysburg, Penn.: Thomas, 1990.

Priest, John M. *Victory without Triumph: The Wilderness, May 6 and 7, 1864.* Shippensburg, Penn.: White Mane, 1996.

R. C. "Gen. Lee at the 'Wilderness.'" *The Land We Love* 5 (October, 1868): 481 – 86.

Rhea, Gordon C. *The Battle of the Wilderness, May 5–6, 1864.* Baton Rouge: Louisiana State University Press, 1994.

Richardson, Rupert Norval; Ernest Wallace; and Adrian N. Anderson. *Texas: The Lone Star State.* Englewood Cliffs, N.J.: Prentice-Hall, 1970.

Roberts, O. M. *Military History of Texas.* Vol. 15 of *Confederate Military History,* edited by Clement A. Evans. Atlanta: Confederate Publishing, 1899. Reprint, Wilmington, N.C.: Broadfoot, 1989.

Robertson, James I., Jr. *Stonewall Jackson: The Man, the Soldier, the Legend.* New York: Macmillan, 1997.

Robertson, Jerome B., comp. *Touched with Valor: Civil War Papers and Casualty Reports of Hood's Texas Brigade.* Edited by Harold B. Simpson. Hillsboro, Tex.: Hill Junior College Press, 1964.

Sears, Stephen W. *George B. McClellan: The Young Napoleon.* New York: Ticknor and Fields, 1988.

———. *To the Gates of Richmond: The Peninsula Campaign.* New York: Ticknor and Fields, 1992.

Sifakis, Stewart. *Compendium of the Confederate Armies: Texas.* New York: Facts on File, 1995.

———. *Who Was Who in the Confederacy.* New York: Facts on File, 1988.

———. *Who Was Who in the Union.* New York: Facts on File, 1988.

Simpson, Harold B. *Gaines' Mill to Appomattox: Waco and McLennan County in Hood's Texas Brigade.* Waco, Tex.: Texian Press, 1963.
——. *Hood's Texas Brigade: A Compendium.* Hillsboro, Tex.: Hill Junior College Press, 1977.
——. *Hood's Texas Brigade: Lee's Grenadier Guard.* Waco, Tex.: Texian Press, 1970. Reprint, Gaithersburg, Md.: Olde Soldier, 1994.
Sommers, Richard J. "Grant's Fifth Offensive at Petersburg : A Study in Strategy, Tactics, and Generalship: The Battle of Chaffin's Bluff, the Battle of Poplar Spring Church, the First Battle of the Darbytown Road, the Second Battle of the Squirrel Level Road, the Second Battle of the Darbytown Road." Master's thesis, Rice University, 1970. Ann Arbor, Mich.: University Microfilms International, 1981. Microfilm.
Stackpole, Edward J. *From Cedar Mountain to Antietam.* Harrisburg, Penn.: Stackpole, 1993.
Stanard, Mary Newton. *Richmond: Its People and Its Story.* Philadelphia: J. B. Lippincott, 1923.
Steere, Edward. *The Wilderness Campaign: The Meeting of Grant and Lee.* 1960. Reprint, Mechanicsburg, Penn.: Stackpole, 1994.
Stevens, John W. *Reminiscences of the Civil War.* Hillsboro, Tex.: Hillsboro Mirror Print, 1902. Reprint, Powhatan, Va.: Derwent, 1982.
Sumrall, Alan K. *Battle Flags of Texans in the Confederacy.* Austin: Eakin Press, 1995.
Symonds, Craig L. *Joseph E. Johnston: A Civil War Biography.* New York: W. W. Norton, 1992.
Taylor, Walter H. *Four Years with General Lee.* Bloomington: Indiana University Press, 1962.
Thomas, Emory M. *Bold Dragoon: The Life of J. E. B. Stuart.* New York: Harper and Row, 1986.
——. *Robert E. Lee.* New York: W. W. Norton, 1995.
Trudeau, Noah Andre. *Bloody Roads South: The Wilderness to Cold Harbor, May–June, 1864.* Boston: Little, Brown, 1989.
——. *Out of the Storm: The End of the Civil War, April–June, 1865.* Boston: Little, Brown, 1994.
Tucker, Glenn. *Chickamauga : Bloody Battle in the West.* Indianapolis: Bobbs-Merrill, 1961. Reprint, Old Saybrook, Conn.: Konecky and Konecky, 1995.
U.S. War Department, comp. *Atlas to Accompany the Official Records of the Union and Confederate Armies.* Washington: Government Printing Office, 1891 – 1895. Reprinted as *The Official Military Atlas of the Civil War,* New York: Gramercy, 1983.
——. *War of the Rebellion: A Compilation of the Official Records of the Union and Confederate Armies.* 128 vols. Washington: Government Printing Office, 1880 – 1901. CD-ROM reprint, Carmel: Guild Press of Indiana, 1996.
Vandiver, Frank. *Jubal's Raid: General Early's Famous Attack on Washington in 1864.* 1960. Reprint, Lincoln: University of Nebraska Press, 1992.
Warner, Ezra. *Generals in Blue.* 1964. Reprint, Baton Rouge: Louisiana State University Press, 1992.
——. *Generals in Gray.* 1959. Reprint, Baton Rouge: Louisiana State University Press, 1987.

Wert, Jeffry D. *General James Longstreet: The Confederacy's Most Controversial Soldier, a Biography.* New York: Simon and Schuster, 1993.

West, John C. *A Texan in Search of a Fight. Being the Diary and Letters of a Private Soldier in Hood's Texas Brigade.* Waco, Tex.: J. S. Hill,1901. Reprint, Baltimore: Butternut and Blue, 1994.

Wheeler, Kenneth W. *To Wear a City's Crown: The Beginnings of Urban Growth in Texas, 1836–1865.* Cambridge: Harvard University Press, 1968.

Wheeler, Richard. *Sword over Richmond: An Eyewitness History of McClellan's Peninsula Campaign.* New York: Harper and Row, 1986.

———. *Witness to Appomattox.* New York: Harper and Row, 1989.

Winkler, Mrs. A. V. *The Confederate Capital and Hood's Texas Brigade.* Austin: Eugene Von Boeckmann, 1894. Reprint, Baltimore: Butternut and Blue, 1991.

Woodworth, Steven E. *A Deep Steady Thunder: The Battle of Chickamauga.* Fort Worth: Ryan Place, 1996.

———. *Six Armies in Tennessee: The Chickamauga and Chattanooga Campaigns.* Lincoln: University of Nebraska Press, 1998.

Wooster, Ralph A. *Lone Start Generals in Gray.* Austin: Eakin, 2000.

———. *Texas and Texans in the Civil War.* Austin: Eakin, 1995.

Wright, Marcus Joseph, comp. *Texas in the War, 1861–1865.* Hillsboro, Tex.: Hill Junior College Press, 1965.

Young, Mrs. M. J. "Fifth Texas Regimental Flag." *Confederate Veteran* 11, no. 3 (March, 1903): 105 – 106.

"Young, Matilda Jane Fuller." *The Handbook of Texas Online.* February 25, 2001 < http://www.tsha.utexas.edu/handbook/online/articles/view/YY/ fyo10.html >.

INDEX

⌣

Page numbers referring to maps appear in *italics*.

ISBN 1-58544-238-0

9 781585 442386

90000

1000444096